T0323752

Global Leadership

John Nirenberg

■ Fast track route to mastering the art of global leadership

■ Covers the key areas of global leadership, from defining the
qualities that distinguish global leadership from
conventional leadership and how a global presence
requires an understanding of your company's impact
overseas, to leading from a distance and understanding
what it takes to make global leadership work

■ Examples and lessons from some of the world's most
successful businesses, including McKinsey, Nokia, Nestlé
and Matsushita, and ideas from the smartest thinkers,
including Warren Bennis, John Kotter, Robert Rosen, Philip
R. Harris, Robert T. Moran and Peter Senge

■ Includes a glossary of key concepts and a comprehensive
resources guide.

>>EXPRESS EXEC.COM<<
essential management thinking at your fingertips

The right of John Nirenberg to be identified as the author of this work has been
asserted in accordance with the Copyright, Designs and Patents Act 1988

First published 2002 by
Capstone Publishing (a Wiley company)
8 Newtec Place
Magdalen Road
Oxford OX4 1RE
United Kingdom
http://www.capstoneideas.com

CIP catalogue records for this book are available from the British Library and the
US Library of Congress

ISBN 1-84112-236-X

This book is printed on acid-free paper

Substantial discounts on bulk quantities of Capstone books are available
to corporations, professional associations and other organizations. Please
contact Capstone for more details on +44 (0)1865 798 623 or (fax) +44
(0)1865 240 941 or (e-mail) info@wiley-capstone.co.uk

Contents

Introduction to ExpressExec

ExpressExec is 3 million words of the latest management thinking compiled into 10 modules. Each module contains 10 individual titles forming a comprehensive resource of current business practice written by leading practitioners in their field. From brand management to balanced scorecard, ExpressExec enables you to grasp the key concepts behind each subject and implement the theory immediately. Each of the 100 titles is available in print and electronic formats.

Through the ExpressExec.com Website you will discover that you can access the complete resource in a number of ways:

» printed books or e-books;
» e-content – PDF or XML (for licensed syndication) adding value to an intranet or Internet site;
» a corporate e-learning/knowledge management solution providing a cost-effective platform for developing skills and sharing knowledge within an organization;
» bespoke delivery – tailored solutions to solve your need.

Why not visit www.expressexec.com and register for free key management briefings, a monthly newsletter and interactive skills checklists. Share your ideas about ExpressExec and your thoughts about business today.

Please contact elound@wiley-capstone.co.uk for more information.

Introduction to Global Leadership

Global leadership is a new concept indicative of the evolution of multinational corporations into stateless entities now functioning with the whole world as their domain. Thus:

» Global leadership requires a uniquely new brand of leadership;
» A sensitivity to corporate behavior, globally, is required.

"I think there are good reasons for suggesting that the modern age has ended. Today, many things indicate that we are going through a transitional period, when it seems that something is on the way out and something else is painfully being born. It is as if something were crumbling, decaying and exhausting itself, while something else, still indistinct, were arising from the rubble."

Vaclav Havel, former President of the Czech Republic[1]

Exxon Mobil is the world's largest global corporation on *Fortune* magazine's list of the world's largest corporations,[2] with sales over $210 billion – $4 billion more than the gross domestic product (GDP) of the world's largest oil-producing country, Saudi Arabia. Exxon Mobil, formerly Exxon, Esso and Standard Oil Company of New Jersey, has been a multinational corporation (MNC) for almost 100 years, with operations virtually everywhere there is a need for petroleum products.

Wal-Mart is the second largest corporation on *Fortune*'s list. It has revenues of more than $193 billion and 1,244,000 employees; half the population of the State of Arkansas in which it was founded almost 40 years ago.

Last on *Fortune*'s list, at number 500, is Sodexho Alliance, a French food services company, with sales over $10 billion – more than the GDP of Cambodia, Cyprus, Fiji, Georgia, Haiti, or Laos (and many others). It could soon equal the $13 billion GDP of neighboring Luxemburg.[3] In short, the world's largest corporations are becoming larger than nation states in economic power, and their influence on the lives of employees and customers all over the globe is growing at Internet speed. Indeed, as the cold war recedes in our memory as a battle between blocks of nation states, a new struggle is emerging between corporations that now roam the earth unencumbered by national boundaries. Because of this and the rising consciousness of the impact of globalization generally, it is vital for managers in large organizations to understand the principles of global leadership. Further, an understanding of global leadership is essential to anyone with career aspirations of managing in this new interdependent, multinational, multicultural world.

A NEW BRAND OF LEADERSHIP

In 1996 Percy Barnevik retired after 10 years as CEO of ABB, an electrical engineering and electronics company that is the world's largest power generation, transmission, and distribution business. He orchestrated the creation of ABB by merging Sweden's Asea and Switzerland's Brown Boveri. At the time it was Europe's biggest cross-border merger, valued at some $30 billion. It was remarkable not only for its size but also for its breadth. By the end of the twentieth century it had 160,000 employees divided among 1300 companies with 5000 profit centers in 140 countries. Yet, there are fewer than 200 employees at the corporate headquarters in Zurich, Switzerland. This extreme decentralization makes it, according to Barnevik, a "multi-domestic organization." Global leadership becomes an essential ingredient of ABB's success. Commenting on global leadership, Barnevik said:

"Global managers are made, not born. This is not a natural process. We are herd animals. We like people who are like us. But there are many things you can do. Obviously, you rotate people around the world. There is no substitute for line experience in three or four countries to create a global perspective. You also encourage people to work in mixed nationality teams. You force them to create personal alliances across borders, which means that sometime you interfere in hiring decisions."

"You also have to acknowledge cultural differences without becoming paralyzed by them ... For example, a Swede may think a Swiss is not completely frank and open, that he doesn't know exactly where he stands. That's a cultural phenomenon. Swiss culture shuns disagreement. A Swiss might say, 'Let's come back to that point later, let me review it with my colleagues.' A Swede would prefer to confront the issue directly. How do we undo hundreds of years of upbringing and education? We don't, and we shouldn't try to. But we do need to broaden understanding."[4]

For the manager working in a large global enterprise aspiring to a leadership position, the challenge to function successfully in different countries and with individuals from myriad cultures is the most important skill to develop. But globalization also has a more surprising impact on the average life that eludes most people's attention.

Cody, Wyoming (population 8835), for example, is an unlikely place for a 16 year old to worry about the impact of globalization. In a simpler time, perhaps as late as the early 1980s, a young athlete in Cody could anticipate a fairly predictable progression from promising junior high school star to local high school starter to state college competitor. If there were any global issues that impacted the local community they might involve migrant workers from Mexico, or the building of strange silos – in the ground instead of on the ground for fodder – from which to launch missiles at the Soviet Union half a planet away. Or perhaps one might have noticed the strange national dress of a locally sponsored exchange student from a Latin-American country or see a foreign tourist or two at the Buffalo Bill museum on the outskirts of town before passing by on their way to Yellowstone National Park.

Today, a promising junior high school athlete would be concerned with competing against the likes of the two Nigerian athletes now at the University of Wyoming and hear about his own coach's scouting expedition to the former Yugoslavia for talented prospects for the basketball team lured by the promise of a collegiate scholarship. Indeed, that young American athlete might now even reconsider his own career prospects in light of the opening of American teams to foreign contenders. Yes, recruiting globally has truly elevated the competition, which now requires world-class performance. Today 12% of the players in the National Basketball Association and 25% of the players in Major League Baseball are foreigners.[5] Not only does it make the competition harder, you don't know where it will come from next.

There is no going back. What was considered an esoteric possibility when we talked about international interdependence in the 1970s is now a very routine reality. All economies are integrating into a larger world market and whether or not you are directly linked to foreign markets and suppliers or influenced by the fluctuation of the Dollar, Yen or Euro, it is simply a matter of time before you will be. And it won't take long. Like 16-year-old basketball players in Cody, Wyoming, feeling the impact of globalization, you too will be influenced by its impact on your business, your professional relationships, and your livelihood.

That's the easy, perhaps obvious part, of the new economic reality brought on by globalization. The harder part to internalize and the subject of this book, is creating the capacity to lead in a global context. Because it is not a skill that comes naturally, as ABB's Barnevik reminded us, global leadership will involve developing an international perspective for building relationships, creating strategy, and executing plans across borders, cultures, and vast distances. Leading effectively in a 24 time-zone marketplace cannot be achieved without varied international experience. And the experience will not be meaningful unless it is considered a time for deliberate development of the skills that will lead to success through the twenty-first century.

There is precedent for this. The industrial revolution that precipitated colonialism saw the creation of a British Empire upon which "the sun never set." The administration of such a far-flung collection of assets, resources and personnel that engulfed about a quarter of the world's land and people was the precursor to the modern MNC. But the MNC is now morphing into a new entity that not only does business overseas but also defines itself more as a global, rather than a national, entity. Clearly MNCs are no longer national instruments. Rather, they are an independent collection of vast commercial interests that operate completely on the world stage. While in their infancy during the cold war, MNCs operated much like the British Empire from a central hub with field personnel sent by and managed from the home office. Today, operations are entirely dispersed and constitute an earth-straddling network of resources connected by a proprietary Internet (or intranet) with satellite and cell-mediated voice and video communications, featuring e-mail, instant messaging and access to all required real time data. Cheap labor, proximity to physical resources, and cheap transportation costs have created a world sourcing challenge to minimize costs, maximize reach to customers, and reduce the time needed to connect the knowledge of needs with their fulfillment anywhere in the world.

In practical terms this means that, for example, it is possible that the design of an Apple computer could take place in California, with engineering specifications sent to a chip fabricator in Taiwan, a desktop casing manufacturer in Hong Kong, a hard drive manufacturer in Singapore, a copper fine-wiring contractor in Chile, for small motor wire shipped to a power source manufacturer in Korea, all to be assembled in Malaysia and forwarded to Guadalajara, Mexico, New Jersey, USA, Vancouver, Canada, Lyon, France, and Johannesburg, South Africa for warehousing and distribution. Meanwhile, programming and call center operations for logistics and customer service would take place outside of Mumbai, India, HR benefits administration would be based in Dublin, and the sales and local customer service would be handled by regional, autonomous sub-headquarters on each continent, while advertising, product support, and training would be located in each market.

Indeed, looking around the average home shows how entrenched we are in a global economic system dominated by multinationals that operate wherever there is a market for their products. Examples might be clothes from Bangladesh, electronics from Japan, wines from France and Chile, furniture from Indonesia and Denmark, Japanese automobiles made in the US, books by US authors published by a German media giant, CDs made in Hong Kong, computer monitors from Taiwan, glasses from China, and newsprint from Canada. Our appetite for products isn't all that drives globalization, however. The companies that create these products (and services – United Airlines, for example, has websites in the local language in each of the 27 countries in which it does business) operate as if the globe were a single market. It is that which distinguishes globalization from simply doing business abroad. And it is that aspect of doing business with so many different people under so many different conditions that raises the stakes for individuals hoping to lead global organizations. Globalization also brings migration: Turks to Germany as "guest workers;" Indians to the Caribbean; Hispanics to North America; Saharan Africans to France. In addition, each nation now experiences a dramatic increase in the numbers of foreign nationals who are transferred to work or study there and who contribute to the overall quality of life before moving on or returning to their homes. There is even a new set of challenges to anyone hoping to exercise leadership at home because of the increasingly diverse nature of the workforce. And, in that regard, understanding the principles of global leadership will be increasingly important to domestic managers who have no greater ambition than to manage locally.

IMPORTANCE OF GLOBAL SENSITIVITIES

Oddly, with the complexity of a global operation, it is easy to lose sight of the intercultural implications of working with so many different individuals representing such varied experiences, values, and expectations. It is this particular aspect that is often overlooked – even considered inconsequential – when all seems to be going well, but often becomes the precise reason for things going badly.

Douglas Ivester, former CEO of Coca-Cola, learned the hard way how cultural sensitivities can be bruised, resulting in long-term issues that directly influenced performance and severely curtailed profitability. In 1999 there was a small contamination of Coca-Cola produced in Belgium and France. It created quite a scare that eventually spread to three other countries, resulting in the recall of 14 million cases of Coke and an overall $35 million hit on corporate profits.[6] While the company's response was slow and defensive, negative public opinion created a virtual boycott of Coke that was unnecessarily severe. After the initial scare "Danny De Man, a bank employee, [said] his 14-year-old daughter, Ann, still 'gets very tired and gets headaches' with even light exercise. He blames it on a bad Coke . . . a doctor representing Coke . . . said that the sulfur compound that contaminated the beverage 'could cause irritation and headaches but it was in such small doses that it would cause no lasting damage,' according to Mr De Man. 'I don't believe him at all because he's been paid by Coca-Cola,' he says. 'We have a saying in Flemish: Whose bread one eats, whose words one speaks.' "[7]

Further problems arose due to the slow response from Ivester. He didn't arrive in Belgium until eight days after several schoolchildren were hospitalized. "As the bans on Coke products continued into June 21, Mr Ivester issued a memo to all of his company's 28,000 employees. The subject was the 'Belgian issue' and it said, among other things, that the company's 'quality control processes in Belgium faltered.' He added: 'I have personally tasted the products and held the packages involved with no adverse reaction.' "

Full-page newspaper advertisements appeared that day in French newspapers, asserting the safety of Coke products and listing a toll-free number for people to call with any safety questions. At the same time, Coca-Cola circulated a toxicologist's report it had commissioned, which concluded that substances found in the products in question were in amounts too small to have caused the symptoms people reported. It fanned rumors, reported in European newspapers, that people who said they got sick were actually experiencing "psychosomatic" illnesses.[8] The next day Coke ran an apology for not having communicated earlier.

Here was a case of a 113-year-old MNC with one of the most valuable and respected brands in the world faltering in its handling of an emergency and compounding it with insensitivity and defensiveness. This was all the more surprising because Coca-Cola was usually so adept at working interculturally, characterized by local ownership of bottling plants, so that in many countries in which it operated, people felt it was their own indigenous soft drink.

The questions about Ivester's performance generally and his handling of this event plus a discrimination suit brought by African-American employees in the US ultimately led to his downfall. Certainly, what derailed Ivester was nothing related to his technical skills but his inability to get along with people. According to leadership professors James O'Toole and Warren Bennis, "Ivester was emotionally inept ... and he couldn't empathize with the personal concerns of others ... a one man band who seldom involved others in big decisions ... "[9]

It is because of this rapidly changing operational environment that organizations need effective global leaders. While many aspects of leadership in a global environment will resemble aspects of leadership as it is generally understood, there are some significant differences that will dramatically affect one's success in the international arena. First is a cultural sensitivity that acknowledges differences. Second, respecting those differences and how they influence behavior among overseas partners, employees, and customers is essential. As George Fisher, retired CEO of Kodak said, "You must capture the hearts and minds of all your employees [and customers] but you must do it differently around the world."[10]

NOTES

1 Remarks at the Liberty Medal ceremony, Philadelphia: July 4, 1994.
2 (2001) "The World's Largest Corporations (Global 500 by the Numbers)." *Fortune*, July 23, F-1–F-44.

3 GDP numbers from *The World Almanac and Book of Facts, 2000*, World Almanac Books, Mahwah, NJ.
4 Data from *Hoover's Global 250: The Stories Behind the Most Powerful Companies on the Planet*, Hoover's Business Press, Austin, TX, 1997 and Kets de Vries, Manfred F.R. and Florent-Treacy, Elizabeth, *The New Global Leaders: Richard Branson, Percy Barnevik and David Simon*, Jossey-Bass, San Francisco, CA, 1999.
5 Goldman, Tom, (2001) "The changing face of sports in America." *Morning Edition*, National Public Radio, Washington, DC, April 25.
6 Deogun, Nikhil, *et al.* (1999) "Cola stains – anatomy of a recall: how Coke's controls fizzled out in Europe – lapses let contaminants into products; PR flubs only made things worse – 'deviation in taste and color'." *The Wall Street Journal*, June 29.
7 Ibid.
8 Hayes, Constance (1999) "When its customers fell ill, a master marketer faltered." *The New York Times*, June 30.
9 Bennis, Warren and O'Toole, James (2000) "Don't hire the wrong CEO." *Harvard Business Review*, May–June.
10 Rosen, Robert H. (2000) "What makes a globally literate leader?" *Chief Executive*, April, 46–8.

Definition of Terms: What is Global Leadership?

Given the global reach of today's organization, leadership is as much about how work gets done as it is about what gets done and who does it.

» The new environment requires a more practical definition of leadership.
» Globalization requires a new appreciation of differences.
» The idea of global leadership is changing.

"Of the US Fortune 500 firms we surveyed, 85 percent do not think they have an adequate number of global leaders, 67 percent of the firms think that their existing leaders need additional skills and knowledge before they meet or exceed needed capabilities."
Research team from Brigham Young University, the University of Western Ontario, and the University of California, Irvine[1]

Leadership is as much about how work gets done as it is about what gets done and who does it. Leadership is clearly being recognized as a widespread social phenomenon necessary for the achievement of a group's collective objectives. It is no longer just an expression of a position in a hierarchy or a chain of command. Thus, leadership is defined as a form of influence and a type of interaction between an initiator and a follower. Leadership is a set of initiatives and responses between people for the purpose of achieving mutual objectives intended to result in collective effectiveness and personal enrichment over time. As such, many different and diverse expressions of leadership are needed in all organizations and at all levels within organizations. In high performance organizations leadership as a function (as opposed to a role) occurs between people regardless of formal titles, position, or job description.

The importance of generalizing the behaviors that constitute leadership, so each person in an organization can develop a more effective influence style and assume the role of "leader" as catalyst, coordinator, or facilitator, when appropriate, will also be emphasized. Undoubtedly this will be a controversial departure from the conventional wisdom that defines leadership simply as what one does when in charge of a project or the performance of a group of people, but unequivocal evidence suggests that organizational success is increasingly determined by adopting precisely this new perspective leadership – especially within knowledge-based and professional organizations.

One of the first accounts of the appearance of this form of leadership was described by Joseph Rost, who began one of the first doctoral level leadership programs in the US at the University of San Diego. "Leadership is an influence relationship among leaders and followers who intend real changes that reflect their mutual purposes."[2] In our current context, in what is becoming known as the knowledge era, he recognized that, at least within formal organizations, the work between people will take the shape of collegial relationships rather than hierarchical ones. In becoming a more collegial enterprise, essentially composed of "volunteers," mutual consent and negotiated agreement will typify decision making, goal setting and performance appraisal. Clearly, leadership in this environment will require the mutual exchange of influence based on perceived common interest, the expertise of the individuals involved, and the conditions impacting the specific objective at hand.

TOWARD A NEW, MORE PRACTICAL DEFINITION OF LEADERSHIP

Of course there are many forms of influence and we shouldn't confuse them. Perhaps in the near future we will develop a more finely tuned lexicon of leadership, where different forms of influence styles will be defined according to the context, the type of organization, and the degree of expertise among the individuals within them. For now, however, I'd like to make a sharp distinction between the conventional wisdom of leadership as "positionship" (regardless of the form of influence) and leadership as a process of mutual interaction, mutual consent, and mutual gain between leader and follower for the good of the organization. If we see influence style as a product of the nature of the power and values disposition of the individual as a continuum of possibilities, as in Table 2.1, we can distinguish several forms of influence. These distinctions result in various behavioral styles used by an individual or a "position holder" within a group – be it at the level of the organization, division, department, *arrondissement*, bureau, shop, etc. With this understanding, however, not all forms of influence should be defined as "leadership" as that behavior is discussed here.

Simply, leadership is the exercise of a particular kind of influence. While we recognize that this perspective is new, we believe it helps us more accurately frame the discussion by being more precise about what we mean when we talk about global leadership within the context of employee-based organizations in a democratic, free-market society. With this approach we clearly reject the Hitlers, Stalins, Pol Pots and Maos of the world as leaders, though surely they were tyrants and dictators. Influential? Yes. But their influence was largely based on

Table 2.1 Forms of influence. (© 2000, John Nirenberg. Used with permission.)

Forms of Influence	Dictator	Owner/boss	Supervisor Administrator (Caretaker)	Manager (transactional)	Leader (transformational)	Partner
Example (public figure)	Mao	Tito	Herbert Hoover	Lyndon Johnson	Charles De Gaulle	Nelson Mandela
Example (business)	Al Dunlap, Sunbeam	Henry Ford, Ford Motor Company	Typical, numerous	Michael Eisner, Walt Disney	Percy Barnevik, ABB	Jack Stack, Springfield Remanufacturing
Use of power	Coercive	Coercive, legitimate	Coercive, reward	Reward, coercive	Identification/ expertise	Expertise, vision/mission
Outcome relative to employer-employee relationship	Obedience	Obedience	Reluctant compliance	Willing compliance	Consent of followers	Shared ownership of process and results
Effectiveness	Possibly in short term	Possibly in stable environment	Likely only in stable environment	Likely only in stable environment	Likely	Highly likely
Beneficiary of enrichment and rewards	Dictator and cronies	Owner/boss	Company	Company, manager, some followers	Company, leader and followers	Everyone

threat, coercion, intimidation, and mass murder to force compliance and to maintain their position of power. They are not considered to be leaders in the sense of that term as it is used here, even though, of course, they had followers – a necessary but not sufficient requirement to be a leader.

The CEO represents a point of contact to the external world of investors, regulators, and the local (sometimes even international) community. His or her role is to facilitate the creation of a vision, a mission, and a strategy to achieve them. It is the CEO to whom most people naturally turn for "leadership." And that individual in exercising leadership – as a process of mutual interaction, mutual consent, and mutual gain between leader and follower for the good of the organization – does so in addition to stewarding the organization. But the act of leadership will also be a functional part of everyone's job who works with other people within any organization. Thus, it is important for leadership skills to be dispersed throughout the organization in order to craft the ability of a diverse workforce to live the vision and achieve the mission of the organization as expected in accordance with its strategy. Leadership is most effective when it results in an organization (unit, department, school, *arrondissement*, etc.) implementing its strategy and reaching its goals, while the experience of work in the organization is satisfying to its employees.

In order to identify best leadership practices, it is therefore important to decide which intended outcomes will be sought in utilizing the leadership form of influence. Remember that the use of leadership as a form of influence doesn't preclude the use of other influence styles such as "boss," but the distinction certainly keeps our conversation more focused when using these concepts. When we are being a "boss," or a "manager," or a "dictator," or a "partner," we should recognize it as such and not simply claim that whatever behavior is exercised by a person with power is "leadership."

A "leadership" influence style focuses on the mobilization of colleagues in a consensual, collective effort to achieve the organization's vision. This may also involve some real managerial constraints. For example, organizations must not only be effective in implementing their strategy, they must also be efficient. Indeed, a profit must accompany its actions and it must be adaptable to external demands for change and internal processes to meet employer and employee needs as well. For our purposes, when we discuss leadership in a global context, we assume an understanding of the managerial imperatives and focus on the contextual and interpersonal, cross-cultural aspects of building relationships and being effective around the world.

GLOBALIZATION REQUIRES OPENNESS TO NEW PERSPECTIVES

The successful management of organizations creates the demand for leadership and the successful act of leadership requires people to become more open to their whole experience of interpersonal interaction in the workplace. In effect each person will need to see more, hear more, understand more – in order to help the organization see and meet the changing needs of customers and employees, and to focus the collective productive intent of their part of the organization on achieving effective results. It is about intelligence – about pushing back personal limitations and being open to new possibilities for creating a better, more enjoyable, more successful organization. As Lee Kun-Hee, chairman, Samsung Electronics, South Korea said, "To effectuate change within groups, we must initiate change within ourselves. You need to know yourself well, your habits, strengths and shortcomings. Questioning yourself thoroughly is the beginning of change."[3] In a global economy this is essential.

Most of all, perhaps, the act of leadership is about building strong positive relationships. The result of effective leadership is ultimately the creation of a seamless partnership between customer, employee, and organizational purpose in order to succeed in the marketplace.

CHANGING THE IDEA OF GLOBAL LEADERSHIP

Prior to the turn of the twenty-first century, global leadership was simply considered leadership if it involved people in more than one country – only rarely was it conceptualized as having unique characteristics, as being different from leadership as that term was commonly understood. At best, it was seen as an international variant of leadership that included a sensitivity to local customs when abroad. British managers would be cautioned to look to the left when crossing streets in the Western hemisphere or told that they couldn't import currency into India or Egypt. Americans were told not to touch Thais on the head for that is taboo. At that superficial level regarding one's awareness of the conventions of doing business abroad, this might have been helpful, but few real distinctions were drawn identifying the unique qualities of leading when working on the global stage. Global leadership requires an active sensitivity to fundamental differences among people that impact the success of influence attempts. It also means having a global framework that informs one's thinking about all aspects of the organization and the people who constitute its essence.

Jack Riechert, retired CEO, Brunswick Corporation, spoke for many when he said "Financial resources are not the problem. We have the money, products and position to be a dominant global player. What we lack are the human resources. We just don't have enough people with the needed global leadership capabilities."[4]

The main aspect of global leadership that differentiates it from one's personal experience of leadership in their home culture is the absolute necessity to deal with people of other cultures as colleagues and peers. And in virtually every country in the non-English-speaking world, working with colleagues means working with groups of people, teams, and networks. As Chilean CEO Guillermo Luksic of the Luksic Group reminds us, "Good leaders don't act alone. They build teams of talented managers, each with a distinct point of view. I don't believe in the term 'personal leadership.' That's why we hire people who work well on teams, stress group participation and know how to seek team input."[5]

Clearly, managing effectively in this new era of globalization, whether it be in a complex international network or a culturally diverse local facility, demands an understanding of the principles of global leadership. One needs to appreciate the cultural differences: not just the differences in conventions regarding how work gets done – but people's underlying belief and behavior systems. In building relationships it is important to become interculturally fluent – able to relate to people no matter where you meet them, and, more importantly for the global leader, work with them toward the accomplishment of mutual goals.

NOTES

1 Gregersen, Hal, Morrison, Allen and Black J. (1998) "Developing leaders for the global frontier." *Sloan Management Review*, Fall, 21-32.

2 Rost, Joseph (1993) *Leadership for the Twenty-first Century*. Praeger, Westport, CT.

3 Rosen, Robert H. (2000) "What makes a globally literate leader?" *Chief Executive*, April, 46-8.

4 Gregersen, Hal, Morrison, Allen and Black, J. (1998) "Developing leaders for the global frontier." *Sloan Management Review*, Fall, 21-32.

5 Rosen, Robert H. (2000) "What makes a globally literate leader?" *Chief Executive*, April, 46-8.

The Evolution of Global Leadership

Global leadership has evolved with the idea of globalization. Both have accelerated with the demise of the cold war.

» Viewing the world as a single place in which to do business requires an understanding of how differences will impact the way one behaves as a leader.

» Globalization will also influence how organizations become effective.

"The driving idea behind globalization is free market capitalism – the more you let market forces rule and the more you open your economy to free trade and competition, the more efficient and flourishing your economy will be. Globalization means the spread of free-market capitalism to virtually every country in the world. Globalization also has its own set of economic rules – rules that revolve around opening, deregulating and privatizing your economy."

Thomas L. Friedman[1]

Global leadership as a unified concept is the result of the confluence of two forces: globalization and leadership. Thus, we will first turn to globalization and then to leadership to explore how these concepts evolved.

THE EVOLUTION OF GLOBALIZATION

We could begin an exploration of the need for global leadership and its meaning by first examining the early trading states for clues to their international and intercultural successes. The Phoenicians might make a convenient starting point, having linked Asian and Greek civilizations over 3000 years ago, expanding westward to what is now southern Spain and northwest Africa. We could look at other civilizations and empires that grew through warfare and conquest as the traditionally favored method for the expansion of their culture and beliefs.

But it is peaceful trade that has most convincingly led the world toward globalization as we know it. And though MNCs have existed for a long time it has only been within the last 10 years from the dissolution of the Soviet Union, the rise of the Internet and the creation of trade blocks that the one-world economic future can be seen.

The current knitting together of national economies into a truly interlocking, not just interdependent, global economic system is accelerating and has already had a profound impact on the way business is conducted, the breadth of managerial vision, and lives of people from Bismarck, North Dakota, to Bergen, Norway, to Ouagadougou, Burkina Faso, to Beijing, China. Witness the development of NAFTA (North American Free Trade Agreement) liberalizing trade between Canada, Mexico, and the US, the EU (European Union) forging the

Euro, a single currency system and open borders among members, and the WTO (World Trade Organization) pushing for a worldwide free trade system with supranational powers to adjudicate and enforce commercial agreements and standards.

Globalization, as we know it, took off in the early 1990s and is most characterized by an extra-national orientation unfettered by the global politics of the cold war that dominated the post Second World War era subjugating MNCs to geopolitical priorities. Indeed, rightly or wrongly, today with the widespread belief that "capitalism has won the war," commercial organizations of our time have been set free through deregulation, privatization, and new technologies to carry the burden of economic growth, political stability, and human progress throughout the world.

GLOBALIZATION TIMELINE

Prelude

» **1901**: Death of Queen Victoria and the height of the British Empire.
» **1944**: Bretton Woods (established the World Bank and International Monetary Fund).
» **1945**: United Nations formed.
» **1947**: GATT (General Agreement on Tariffs and Trade) formed (to discuss trade barriers and trade-related disputes).

Current phase

» **1989**: Destruction of the Berlin Wall.
» **1991**: Soviet Union Collapses.
» **1992**: World Wide Web (graphical user interface for the Internet) developed.
» **1993**: Maastricht Treaty establishes EU (European Union) (free movement of goods, services and people within member countries).
» **1995**: Netscape Navigator, the first commercial Internet browser, released.
» **1994**: NAFTA (North American Free Trade Agreement) set up.
» **1995**: A watershed year:
   » WTO (World Trade Organization) administers GATT and serves as a supranational regulatory body;

» Royal Dutch/Shell is embroiled in two international incidents that are warning shots for the anti-globalization movement (more in Chapter 5), namely the Brent Spar oil rig demolition and their support of abuses by the Nigerian security forces against environmental dissidents; and

» publication of *When Corporations Rule the World* criticizing the coming globalization by a 30-year veteran of international aid and development.

» **1999**: Globalization backlash taken to the streets of Seattle, Washington State (USA), meeting of the WTO.

» **1999**: Publication of *The Lexus and the Olive Tree*, popularizing the inevitable impact of globalization.

» **2001**: Disruption of G-8 (Group of Eight – the US, Japan, Germany, France, Italy, UK, Canada, and Russia – who meet to discuss currency values and other mutual global economic matters) meeting in Genoa, Italy, by 150,000 demonstrators protesting against globalization.

THE EVOLUTION OF GLOBAL LEADERSHIP

"We look for highly educated and flexible, open-minded people who can work across borders, who can be international and local at the same time, and who are naturally culturally sensitive; we want people who can think beyond cultural differences."

Helen Alexander, managing director, The Economist Group[2]

The underlying principles of effective leadership are themselves virtually as old as the written word, and ancient civilizations codified these concepts eons ago.

It is written in the book of instruction by Ptah-Hotep, an Egyptian Pharaoh, to his offspring, as early as 2700BCE, that: "If thou art a leader commanding the affairs of the multitude, seek out for thyself every beneficial deed ... Truth is great, and its effectiveness is lasting ... If thou art one to whom petition is made, be calm as thou listenest to what the petitioner has to say. Do not rebuff him before he has said that for which he came ...."[3]

In another manuscript of instruction from ancient Egypt, it is written, "Proclaim thy business without concealment ... One ought to say plainly what one knoweth and what one knoweth not."[4]

Sun Tzu, writing in *The Art of War* around 500BCE offers words of wisdom as valid in the West today as in his homeland, ancient China: "If wise, a commander is able to recognize changing circumstances ... If sincere, his men will have no doubt of the certainty of rewards and punishments. If humane, he loves mankind, sympathizes with others and appreciates their industry and toil. If courageous, he gains victory. . ."[5]

In India, in the fourth century BCE, Vishnugupta wrote *Arthasastra*, an enquiry into the act of leadership. Regarding the qualifications of a state officer, he wrote, the candidate for high office should be:

". . .well trained in arts, possessed of foresight, wise, of strong memory, bold, eloquent, skillful, intelligent, possessed of enthusiasm, dignity and endurance, pure in character, affable, firm in loyal devotion, endowed with excellent conduct, strength, health and bravery, free from procrastination and ficklemindedness, affectionate and free from such qualities as excite hatred and enmity – these are the qualifications of a ministerial officer."[6]

Islam, too has spoken about capable leadership. "The best leaders are those who love the people and are in turn loved by them ... The rulers should defend and honor the property, the life and dignity of all their subjects irrespective of class or creed."[7]

Clearly, the wisdom of modern leadership is the latest link in a long chain of insights first identified by the ancients and refined by each generation thereafter. They indeed feel universal and timeless. Yet, this attention to traits and emulating the formal leaders of the day had great limitations. Even Machiavelli's *The Prince*,[8] perhaps the most famous and enduring piece of advice to a leader-ruler, handed down to us from its sixteenth-century origins in Florence, offers insights on the politics and trials one faces as a leader but clearly does not address the idea that leadership itself can be a shared and widely distributed function throughout an organization. After all, *The Prince* was indeed written as guidance to absolute rulers.

The later half of the twentieth century witnessed an explosion in our understanding of leadership – its responsibilities as well as the competencies necessary to be effective. The father of modern management, Peter Drucker, has written a small library of books that emphasize the complexity and the need for a systematic approach to the execution of the role of management and leadership. Though to him a leader is simply one who has followers, he sees many of what we consider leadership functions to be essential elements of the managerial role without the mystique and romance that seems to have enveloped the concept in recent years. In his most thorough and encyclopedic treatment of the responsibilities of management he has said that: "Managers in the traditional sense will have to be able to move into situations where they are not superiors, indeed, into situations they are the 'juniors' to nonmanagers on a team or a task force. Conversely, career professionals without managerial function or title in the traditional sense will have to be able to be team leaders or task force leaders. The traditional separation between managers and nonmanagers will increasingly become a hindrance and inappropriate."[9]

In his usual prescient way, Drucker anticipated the need for each person to take responsibility, lead when he or she is in a position to contribute, and follow others when appropriate. Leadership is a part of the managerial role and not separate from it as some respected scholars have suggested of late. As a manager, one is to lead colleagues, whether peers or subordinates, to success and effectiveness. And it is this that leadership teaching and practice has devoted the last 20 years to understanding. But it has only been over the last 10 years of "diversity" and the idea that influencing skills should be widespread that we can see the emergence of a special category of leadership called global leadership.

While leadership has been understood as being exercised among "people like us" it must now, for the first time on a large scale, be practiced with an appreciation of succeeding with "people not like us."

Today, then, global leadership is a young field that synthesizes management, culture studies, communications technology, and social systems dynamics among others, and stresses not the acquisition of specialized knowledge *per se* but the experience of success in cross-cultural situations. It is therefore a field that understandably values the introspection and reflection of a person who has traveled widely, and worked with "people not like us." To develop the proper fluency in interpersonal, cross-cultural dynamics one must quite simply do it. And that means placing oneself in a situation to encounter people from different backgrounds, cultures, and countries.

CULTURE'S CONSEQUENCES

In 1980, Geert Hofstede, while dean of Semafor Senior Management College and director of the Institute for Research on International Cooperation in Arnhem, The Netherlands, published the results of his study of IBM employees in 40 countries. Though limited to IBM, his insights became a benchmark for further research and established a model that remains the basis for learning the contingencies of cross-cultural work.[10]

He identified four primary behavioral influences that should help global leaders understand their interpersonal environment. Though his work has been controversial, his insights have proven valuable to global leaders.

The dimensions are as follows.

1 **Power distance** – the degree of legitimate differences in the possession and use of power. The range may be from completely egalitarian (low) to reflecting a caste system (high).
2 **Uncertainty avoidance** – the degree to which a person avoids ambiguity and uncertainty. The range may be from the ability to function without rules, defined procedures, and specific expectations (low) to the need for specificity and the comfort found in the rules, procedures, and expectations of a bureaucracy (high).
3 **Individualism vs. Collectivism** – the extent to which a person tends to be concerned about either himself (individualism) or the welfare of the group (collectivism).
4 **Masculinity vs. Femininity** – the adherence to a set of sex role patterns unrelated to gender but to qualities associated with a role. Thus assertiveness, goal orientation, measurement, toughness, strength are considered masculine, while nurturance, relationship building, value orientation is considered characteristic of femininity.

Though generalizations from national studies applied to individual situations are prone to various difficulties such as excessive stereotyping, these dimensions help one focus attention on how relationships unfold and underlying cultural values are expressed.

GLOBAL LEADERSHIP AND ORGANIZATIONAL EFFECTIVENESS (THE GLOBE STUDY)

Building on Hostede's work in 1993, Robert J. House at the University of Pennsylvania, US, began what became a continuing 62-country study specifically to understand the cultural contingencies on leadership around the world. The GLOBE study defined leadership as "the ability to motivate, influence and enable individuals to contribute to the effectiveness of organizations of which they are members."[11] It also expanded the conceptualization of culture to nine dimensions and their influence on leadership behavior. Their additional dimensions include the following.

5 **Humane orientation** – meaning fair, caring and kind to others. A great deal is high on this dimension and little is low.
6 **Assertiveness** – the degree to which people are assertive, aggressive, and confrontational. A lot is high, little is low.
7 **Gender egalitarianism** – the degree to which a culture minimizes gender inequality. A lot of effort to close the gender gap is a high degree of this dimension; little attempt to close the gap is low. (This replaces Hofstede's Masculinity vs. Femininity scale.)
8 **Future orientation** – the extent to which people delay gratification, plan, and invest in the future. Once again, the more future orientation the higher the score.
9 **Performance orientation** – the degree to which performance improvement and excellence are encouraged and rewarded.

House reported that: "As hypothesized, the value based leader syndrome (formerly referred to as charismatic leadership: visionary, inspirational, decisive, performance oriented, with high integrity, enthusiastic, positive, encouraging, morale booster, motive arouser, confidence builder, dynamic, and convincing) is viewed as favorable in all countries ... and highly favorable in almost all countries ... It appears that we may have found a leader behavior that is viewed as both universally desirable and effective – a universal etic! [a general, accepted quality]."

Three other leader behavior syndromes were found to be culturally contingent, i.e. viewed favorably or unfavorably, depending on the culture under investigation. More specifically, bureaucratic-collectivistic leadership and autocratic leadership are viewed unfavorably in cultures that score high on future orientation and favorably in cultures that score low on future orientation.

Future orientation, performance orientation, humane orientation, and bureaucratic-collective orientation were found to be universally valued. Power oriented leadership (autocratic and status seeking) was universally devalued, but gender inequality and assertiveness (analogous to Hofstede's masculinity dimension), and uncertainty avoidance were found to vary substantially by culture.

The contributions of these two studies are valuable. They give us a framework with which to examine our intercultural experience and a hint of those leadership behaviors that seem likely to succeed or fail due to the dynamics of culture.

LEADERSHIP TIMELINE

Prelude

Moral character and duty, primary aspects of leadership in the ancient world:

» **2700BCE**: First-known management book (Egypt).
» **500BCE**: Sun Tzu (China).
» **400BCE**: Vishnugupta (India).
» **AD900**: Alfarabi (Islam).

Power and manipulation as a means of maintaining one's leadership:
» **1510**: Machiavelli (Florence).

Current phase

» **1900**: Traditional search for and reporting on traits, the qualities thought necessary to lead.
» **1911**: Frederick Taylor's *Scientific Management*[12] encourages separation of management from work (thinking from doing). Leads to efficiencies but disconnects people from taking responsibility for their work.

» **1950**: Behavioral Styles research seeks to understand the impact of what a leader does, not just who he is; leadership classified as attention to task and relationships.

» **1967**: Contingency model of leadership. Managers must alter their behavior in accordance with changing circumstances.

» **1974**: Peter Drucker publishes *Management: Tasks, Responsibilities, Practices*.

» **1980**: Hofstede publishes *Culture's Consequences*, first comprehensive global leadership study.

» **1990**: Leadership shifts focus from power to influence.

» **1991**: Need for new global leadership emerges with demise of Soviet Union and rise of market-based economies worldwide.

» **1993**: Rise of virtual organizations.

» **1993+**: GLOBE (Global Leadership and Organizational Effectiveness) 62-country study identifies key aspects of leadership across cultures.

» **1997**: Rise of remote teams, network-based organizational structures and truly global organizations benefiting from a worldwide supracultural convergence around western (though primarily US) influences: global brands, CNN, MTV, ATMs and worldwide electronic financial markets. Point brought home with rolling global financial crisis due to speculative currency trading.

NOTES

1 Friedman, Thomas L. (1999) *The Lexus and the Olive Tree: Understanding Globalization.* Farrar Straus Giroux, New York, p. 8.

2 Rosen, Robert H. (2000) "What makes a globally literate leader?" *Chief Executive*, April, 46–8.

3 Wilson, John A. (1951) *The Culture of Ancient Egypt*. University of Chicago Press, Chicago, p. 84.

4 Adapted from Erman, A. (1927) *The Literature of the Ancient Egyptians*, trans. Alward M. Blackman, E.P. Dutton and Co., New York, p. 55.

5 Sun Tzu (1971) *The Art of War*, trans. Samuel B. Griffith. Oxford University Press, New York, p. 65.

6 Vishnugupta (1956) *Arthasastra*, trans. S. Shamasastry. Sri Raghuveer Printing, Mysore, India, p. 14.

7 Syed Al Atas Hussain (1973) *Siapa Yang Saleh*. Pustaka Nasional, Singapore.

8 Machiavelli, Nicolo (1967) *The Prince*. Penguin, London.

9 Drucker, Peter (1974) *Management: Tasks, Responsibilities, Practices*. Harper & Row, New York, p. 392.

10 Hofstede, Geert (1984) *Culture's Consequences*. Sage Publications, Thousand Oaks, CA.

11 House, Robert J. "A Brief History of GLOBE," see http://www.mg mt3.ucalgary.ca/eb/globe.nsf/index

12 Taylor, Frederick (1911) *The Principles of Scientific Management*. Harper & Row, New York.

The E-Dimension

The Internet has changed everything and has been the key reason that globalization has occurred so rapidly.

- » Given the global reach of organizations and their need to create a unified supranational culture and to communicate instantaneously, an Internet-based communications protocol will require people to exercise their leadership skills in a totally new environment.
- » A global playing field has also meant that organizing for a decentralized world is a necessity.
- » Global leaders will also need to master the skills to succeed from a distance – with little face-to-face opportunities to build rapport and communicate.

"This new arena for sense making and connection has profound effects as it overcomes geographical, cultural and traditional forms of thinking, behaving and creating meaning."

Richard A. Ogle[1]

Contemporary globalization involves a new perception of the world. No longer do we simply send out branch officers to do business overseas. Today, companies become global when they conceptualize their domain as congruent with that of the planet. The electronic (e-)dimension involves use of satellite communications for in-company live video and voice communications to offices, suppliers, and customers anywhere in the world; use of the intranet, to facilitate shared information through e-mail and support from anywhere on the organization's network; and the use of PDAs (personal digital assistants) to enable individuals to communicate data, and access organizational information via in-house databases from anywhere on the planet at any time.

The e-dimension is primarily expressed through the Internet and e-mail. Though the first level of impact is the exchange of information with people anywhere on the globe, its greatest value may be in helping to forge leadership from a distance.

Given the global reach of organizations, their need to create a unified supranational culture and to communicate instantaneously, an Internet-based communications protocol will require people to exercise their leadership skills in a totally new environment with various new hazards. For example, some people claim that it is the non-verbal language that creates the most potent meaning in any communications. This is why face-to-face meetings are so important. To get a "feel" for the person behind the message – the intonation in the voice, the posture, the movement of the eyes, and facial expressions – one uses all the spontaneous data presented in a face-to-face encounter to evaluate the meta messages. That is difficult from a distance even within one's own culture but is infinitely more complex and fraught with difficulties when it involves communicating by e-mail across cultures.

Though it might appear to make communicating easier, it may only make misunderstanding ensue that much faster. Both parties to e-mail face difficulties in understanding when supportive visual clues, repetition, emphasis, and enquiry are absent. These aspects of communication that are present in face-to-face encounters are frequently missing but essential to include when communicating from a distance. This requires participants to the communication process to be very careful in choosing words, providing more detail and explanatory remarks, emphasizing the consequences and expectations surrounding the message and being open for further discussion, clarification, and refinement to ensure understanding.

LEADERSHIP IN THE INTERNET ERA

If the impact of the Internet is obvious, unavoidable, and demanding our adaptation, the implications for leadership behavior inside organizations are equally as revolutionary and transformational. An Internet mindset must begin with the willingness to alter familiar patterns of human behavior – some seemingly hardwired into our makeup. In particular, people must consider new ways to communicate, build trust, share knowledge and experience, work together, and create a mutual understanding of their reality. Thus, the new Internet era requires that global leaders become fully intentional – deliberate in their processes, inclusive of the contributions of each colleague, and responsive to all stakeholders.

This new environment now demands teamwork, collaboration, a distribution of power to those closest to its required application, and accountability to one another based on performance, expertise, and creativity freely used for the benefit of the group. The measure of success in the Internet era is defined by outcomes not obedience. Controls are to ensure the appropriate utilization of resources toward meeting objectives, not conformity to a job description. Indeed, job descriptions become obsolete in an unpredictable world. These internal changes are necessary to successfully match the demands of the external world of constant change, innovation, and hyper-competitiveness.

The Internet has changed everything. The immediate impact of requiring organizational efficiencies and an ability to innovate quickly is to force the dismantling of rigid hierarchies and conventional protocols. They are being replaced by networks of self-managing teams with access to whatever information they may need in order to respond as quickly as possible to customers and colleagues alike. But this new environment requires an entirely new understanding of what it means to lead and who should play that role. Indeed, while achievement and success in using specialized technical skills led one up a career ladder, while being expected to lead at each step, today the challenge of leadership requires an expertise and fluency in people and communications skills that must include an ability to build trust throughout the network.

While technological, logistical, communications, and supporting infrastructure from fiber-optic cables and communications satellites to state of the art industrial parks and the availability of educated professional employees worldwide has made globalization possible, distance leadership becomes the force that makes it all work. Mastering the communications technologies that include groupware, remote Internet-based meeting and archiving software, virtual whiteboards, and document sharing – perhaps all included in a knowledge management system – is crucial to exercise influence and for building the contact necessary for trust, commitment, and cooperation to flourish.

But the very complexity of this arrangement requires the power of a network, itself driven by decentralized, self-managing teams that require a high level of professionalization, well-established working relationships, at least occasionally meeting face-to-face, and the ability to manage the network for the mutual gain of the participants, the organization, and its customers. And, of course, all of this must reflect the instantaneous nature of the Net.

Typically, a global organization will utilize virtual teams to conduct much of its business. At the very least, a network of individuals will be assembled from around the world to work together on a specific problem and then disband. These teams will frequently come and go as the needs of the organization and each of its components utilizes its own resources on a global basis. The intranet will allow a salesperson in Senegal to enquire about a new product design being engineered in France or a manufacturing schedule for its shipment to Martinique.

BUILDING SUCCESS FROM A DISTANCE

There are several keys to remember in leading a team or network from a distance. First, be thorough in what you communicate. Don't forget that e-mail allows for the transmission of documentation. So, when in doubt, distribute any materials that would be directly helpful to the issues at hand. Second, perhaps not so obvious, err on the side of inclusiveness and open communication. Be careful about the use of "bccs" (blind courtesy copies) and acknowledge everyone's contributions. Liberal use of names, unless you know it to be unwanted, is preferable and more so when leading at a distance because distance is too frequently perceived as being "out of sight, out of mind." Furthermore, building trust and allaying people's anxieties that are aroused by not being in touch require more communication – reminders, acknowledgements, and invitations to contribute.

Presenting feedback and evaluations are perhaps the most difficult to do at a distance, but are sometimes required. They should be handled with utmost delicacy and perhaps at this point done via telephone and/or videoconferencing. Teleconferences are used more frequently for general purpose meetings, but they too may be prone to difficulties due to cross-cultural communications breakdowns. The technology is good but not great. Pacing of a conversation, idioms, vocabulary differences, and accents frequently diminish understanding. Follow up with an e-mail summation of the discussions and a recap of any commitments made.

The e-dimension of global leadership truly reduces interpersonal relationships to basics and requires that an extra effort be made to be conscious of the limitations of both e-mail and teleconferences.

THE E-DIMENSION AS TIME MACHINE

There is simply no question that e-mail, the Internet, fax, and fairly low telephone rates makes organizing a network globally a common occurrence that not only saves travel costs but also acts as a time machine, saving enormous time on planes, in hotels, and waiting between action and response. An international trade conference hosted by KOC University in Istanbul, Turkey, was developed by a program committee in Tel Aviv, Israel, Montreal, Canada, Philadelphia and San Jose, USA, with a newsletter editor in London for a document that eventually was printed in and shipped from Athens, Greece. These activities were all handled via e-mail. Travel arrangements were handled by an intercontinental committee that booked flights with special conference partner airlines through a website accepting payment in local currencies. Factory tours and conference entertainment were created with an organization in Istanbul with conference advisors meeting by teleconference during the final month to make all necessary choices regarding events, menus, and equipment. Participants were enrolled in a pre- and post-conference discussion group on a listserve to generate interest in, and an understanding of, the background for many of the presentations that were featured at the conference. All of this was accomplished with only one face-to-face meeting of the entire planning committee and conference directorate, which took place at the annual conference the year before!

Thus, the conference chair and all sub-committee organizers were connected solely by e-mail, Internet, and telephone, and all tasks were fulfilled through this virtual network without needing one day away from home. Each monthly, then bi-weekly online meeting was announced by full color images of Istanbul sent in agenda notes. The excitement and interest in the conference was maintained throughout the year, at least among the organizers, through the imaginative presentation of the city, hot-links (embedded web addresses in e-mail correspondence, not spicy sausages!) to audio/video resources about the conference-related topics, sponsors and entertainment.

The success was of course due to the contributions of on-site facilities organizers, program coordinators, newsletter editors, and myriad sub-committee representatives, all taking the initiative as and when appropriate, and all following the lead of others cooperatively, to make each person's responsibility a success. All were genuinely able to share in the success of the event and all experienced a real sense of achievement through the power of exercising leadership from a distance.

MAKING VIRTUAL TEAMS WORK

- If the team is working on complex issues and taking a long period of time, it is essential to meet in person at least once to get to know one another and become comfortable with the expectations of each of the members.

» Be clear about what the team needs to accomplish together and what aspects can be achieved by individuals working alone.

» Discuss how you will work together. What is an OK time frame for responses to questions? How long will a discussion go on? Will there be round-the-clock monitoring of discussion threads or will one be expected to participate in discussions during usual business hours, etc.?

» Build consensus through the encouragement of each individual's participation.

» Remember, when global leadership is everyone's responsibility, develop high performance expectations for each participant on the team.

» Conclude the project with an appropriate ceremony that at least acknowledges each person's time and effort.[2]

» Don't forget to set up guidelines for the group's Netiquette - the appropriate manner in which team members will communicate on the Net.

NOTES

1 Ogle Richard A., *The Revolutionary Mind*. Forthcoming.
2 Heavily adapted from Katzenbach, Jon and Smith, Douglas (2001) "Virtual teaming," *Forbes*, May 21, 48–51.

The Global Dimension

Globalization has stimulated a backlash due to the impact it has already had on cultures and behavior worldwide.

» There is an organizational challenge to become more responsive to the varied needs of foreign governments and peoples.
» There is also a personal challenge to develop the skills and understanding to work with others of any culture in the achievement of organizational objectives.
» Each global manager will need to develop an appreciation of the triple bottom line: concern for profits, the environment, and social justice.

"Cultural awareness starts not just in bridging culture. It starts by respecting the other person's opinion, by being open to others' ideas and trying to see how they blend with your own beliefs."
Leo Van Wijk, president and CEO, KLM Royal Dutch Airlines [1]

There are many implications of the rapid globalization now taking place for people hoping to become global leaders. First there is the matter of what it will mean to be a citizen of the world. Second, given that intercultural fluency is not present at birth, how shall leaders be prepared for a global future?

THE ORGANIZATIONAL CHALLENGE TO GLOBALIZATION

With nation states seeming to dissolve with the end of the cold war into mere custodians of government services while borderless global enterprises arise without domestic loyalties, there is a growing fear that their unchecked power will not bring a general improvement to the world's people, but will in fact increase the divide between the haves and the have-nots.

Consider these – Seattle: World Trade Association meeting; Washington: World Bank and International Monetary Fund meetings; Davos: World Economic Forum meeting; Quebec: Summit of the Americas meeting to discuss a Free Trade Association of the Americas; Genoa: G-8 Summit 2001. All of these venues became sites for volatile demonstrations against globalization and free trade. This backlash has profound consequences for individual companies; particularly those insensitive to cultural contingencies abroad.

Though corporations have been scouring the world for cheap sources of labor and a lax regulatory environment in the name of pursuing competitive advantage, cultural insensitivity throughout the process has raised consumer consciousness about what is reasonable in an unfettered market economy. But as corporations gain because of a better tax position, cheap labor, an absence of environmental regulations, and global sourcing, consumers have become outraged at the deplorable impact of this behavior on poor nations around the world. This is most in evidence in the textile industry, diamond mining, and other labor intensive production processes. Scenes of child labor in sweatshops, abuse of female assembly line workers, and the devastation of the environments near the workplaces have all caused outrage among the customers who benefited most. This backlash has caused serious damage to several MNCs (multinational corporations).

Nike, the US-based athletic shoe and apparel company, was built on the concept of worldwide outsourcing. At its founding in the 1970s, Nike manufactured its goods in Japan and today, using a network of contract manufacturers brokered by middlemen, Nike products are made in 600 factories from Saipan in the Northern Marianas, South Pacific, to Indonesia to Vietnam to China. While brokering production through middlemen, Nike was able to claim innocence to a series of exploitive labor practices and environmental hazards at those manufacturing sites. It first blamed the middlemen for the circumstances of employment and the local mistreatment of workers; but, under enormous pressure, Nike reluctantly agreed to cooperate with a growing number of interest groups seeking a more "socially responsible" position from them. Indeed, Nike has become the focus of several protest groups formed by its traditional and most ardent customers – college students. The protest organizers formed United Students Against Sweatshops and a Workers Rights Consortium of colleges to pressure Nike, as well as other overseas clothing manufacturers, to audit the conditions under which their products are made.[2]

Phil Knight, the billionaire founder and CEO of Nike, much like CEOs and companies such as Nestlé in the 1970s, simply took a strategy of first, claiming ignorance; second, being defensive; third, reluctantly agreeing to self-monitoring; fourth, becoming cooperative with third party investigators. But at no time did it admit wrongdoing or take the initiative in rectifying the situation. This general approach was quite familiar to CEOs, much like their colonialist predecessors, who merely perceived the world's peoples and resources as instruments of their profit seeking. A more sophisticated approach – one in line with the demands of their critics – is for companies to adopt the CERES[3] principles regarding environmental stewardship for a sustainable future and, for example, the Code of Labor Practices established by the European Clean Clothes Campaign, headquartered in The Netherlands.[4]

As an example of a global company that has attempted to address the twin concerns of labor and environmental fairness, Starbucks has joinèd with TransFair USA to offer "fair trade certified coffee in over 2000 stores in the United States. Fair Trade seeks to improve the lives of coffee growers by ensuring that they receive a guaranteed fair price for their harvest. This helps them afford basic healthcare, education and housing for their families and farms."[5]

THE ANNUS MIRABILIS:1995

The year 1995 was pivotal in the rising public consciousness of the non-economic impact of globalization. And it was Royal Dutch/Shell that had the great misfortune of providing the example of what can go wrong when meaning well. In that year they were first confronted with a challenge from environmentalists who eventually forced the company to abandon its plans for scrapping a North Sea oil platform at sea. Instead, they agreed to tow it to Norway for dismantling. Though Shell actually had economics and science on its side, public opinion was taken aback by the thought of using the bottom of the ocean as a waste disposal dump for a corporation that could easily afford the cost of recycling it. Not only was Shell humiliated by its reversal in the face of a campaign organized by the environmental activists of the nearly bankrupt Greenpeace organization of The Netherlands, but so was John Major, then prime minister of the UK. Major had vocally supported Shell and, for a variety of reasons, found himself only two days later losing a vote of confidence in his Conservative party leadership.

The second situation was more onerous. Shell has been pumping oil from Nigeria for over a generation and still has a very solid franchise there. In part, Shell's good standing was due to their ability to work with the dominant political forces – as would be expected. A group of political dissidents was objecting to the environmental damage being done in the process of extracting the oil and Ken Saro-Wiwa, author and a Nobel Peace Prize nominee, and an outspoken member of the group, earned harsh reprisals from the security forces. He and eight others were tried for murder, convicted by a military court, and all nine were hanged. Worldwide appeals, including those from John Major and Nelson Mandela, were not able to stay their execution. Human rights advocates immediately accused Shell of supporting the security forces and not using their influence to avoid this outrageous travesty of justice.

Peter Schwartz and Blair Gibb summarized the impact of Shell's silence:

> "On a superficial level, it is possible to say that these events had no short-term effect on the company – at the end of the year, its stock price and profits were at record highs. On a deeper level, the experience had a profound effect. A few markets saw violent protests, attacks on Shell retail outlets, and company boycotts. There was widespread comment from the press and public to the effect that Shell's behavior exemplified the stereotype of the irresponsible, indeed evil, multinational. Internally, employees used to being respected for their professionalism and responsibility wrestled with the shock of finding themselves blamed for the tragedies – even their children were being harassed at school."[6]

The case of Royal Dutch/Shell is most ironic since they maintain a long and prosperous reign as one of the world's biggest oil companies, with roots stretching back to the nineteenth century, but it was Shell's corporate planning department that achieved cult status for doing things right. It was their development of a scenario planning process that helped it avoid the ravages of the oil crisis in the 1970s, and earned it a reputation for organizational and intercultural savvy.

By way of contrast: "At Canon, we have put *kyosei* at the heart of our business credo." *Kyosei* is "a spirit of cooperation, in which individuals and organizations live and work together for the common good. A company that is practicing *kyosei* establishes harmonious relations with its customers, its suppliers, its competitors, the government with which it deals, and the natural environment."[7]

The five stages of corporate *kyosei*, according to Ryuzaburo Kaku, chairman emeritus of Canon, the 141st largest MNC in the world, according to *Business Week*[8], are as follows.

» First, tend to your economic survival, the quite familiar bottom line.
» Second, cooperate with labor. Understand you share the same fate.
» Third, cooperate outside the company. Become a partner in solving local problems, partner with competitors, and positively respond to customers and suppliers.

» Fourth, become a global activist. Cooperate with foreign companies and governments by building facilities and a presence overseas contributing to the common good.

» Fifth, encourage others, governments and interest groups, to rectify imbalances so the world economic system is fair to all.

The actions of a company such as Canon, the 70-year-old, $25 billion (revenue) company with 86,000 employees is no small example of what is possible when the belief system tends toward cooperation and harmony instead of exploitation and unilateral gains. Royal Dutch/Shell and Canon thus represent two extremes of corporate global consciousness.

THE PERSONAL CHALLENGE OF GLOBALIZATION

"The Jack Welch of the future cannot be like me. I spent my entire career in the United States. The next head of General Electric will be somebody who spent time in Bombay, in Hong Kong, in Buenos Aires. We have to send our best and brightest overseas and make sure they have the training that will allow them to be the global leaders who will make GE flourish in the future."

Jack Welch, speech at GE, spring, 1997.[9]

(It is worth noting that Welch's hand-picked successor, Jeffrey Immelt, has indeed not spent time overseas though the sentiment is still a valid concern for an increasing number of companies intent on working in the global arena.)

Clearly, the personal challenge for leaders is to balance the acquisition of the technical skills required to navigate the hierarchy and the international experience that will prepare them for leadership in a global organization. In the US today there is a recognition of the importance of international experience as indicated by Jack Welch's quote above, but it does not yet seem to be a defining requirement for the top post. Indeed, 25% of all American managers leave their companies after an overseas assignment. Admittedly their departure is for a variety of reasons, but one important factor is their having been out of the political system in the home office, which diminishes their prospects for climbing the corporate ladder. Out of sight, out of mind is too frequently the treatment they get once they board the plane overseas. Thus, it is important to understand the paradox: overseas experience is increasingly important in a global economy but one must redouble one's efforts to keep contacts and a support network alive in the home office or lose out in promotions there.

This problem sometimes occurs in other cultures. The Japanese are famous for treating returning expatriates as somehow tainted by the experience, though today that is changing – especially among the largest companies.

Europeans are much more comfortable with the international exposure required for leadership in global organizations, especially since they are much more likely to be immersed in a multicultural and multilingual environment from birth. Nevertheless, the challenge remains: one must get the international experience to learn the personal and emotional dimensions of working in different cultures with different values and mindsets; but must also be very mindful of developing the requisite skills to maintain a supportive network at home.

THE CERES (COALITION FOR ENVIRONMENTALLY RESPONSIBLE ECONOMIES) PRINCIPLES OF ENVIRONMENTAL SUSTAINABILITY

By adopting these Principles, we publicly affirm our belief that corporations have a responsibility for the environment, and must conduct all aspects of their business as responsible stewards of the environment by operating in a manner that protects the Earth. We believe that corporations must not compromise the ability of future generations to sustain themselves.

We will update our practices constantly in light of advances in technology and new understandings in health and environmental science. In collaboration with CERES, we will promote a dynamic process to ensure that the Principles are interpreted in a way that accommodates changing technologies and environmental realities. We intend to make consistent, measurable progress in implementing these Principles and to apply them to all aspects of our operations throughout the world.

1. Protection of the biosphere

We will reduce and make continual progress toward eliminating the release of any substance that may cause environmental damage to the air, water, or the earth or its inhabitants. We will safeguard all habitats affected by our operations and will protect open spaces and wilderness, while preserving biodiversity.

2. Sustainable use of natural resources

We will make sustainable use of renewable natural resources, such as water, soils, and forests. We will conserve non-renewable natural resources through efficient use and careful planning.

3. Reduction and disposal of wastes

We will reduce and where possible eliminate waste through source reduction and recycling. All waste will be handled and disposed of through safe and responsible methods.

4. Energy conservation

We will conserve energy and improve the energy efficiency of our internal operations and of the goods and services we sell. We will make every effort to use environmentally safe and sustainable energy sources.

5. Risk reduction

We will strive to minimize the environmental, health and safety risks to our employees and the communities in which we operate through safe technologies, facilities and operating procedures, and by being prepared for emergencies.

6. Safe products and services

We will reduce and where possible eliminate the use, manufacture or sale of products and services that cause environmental damage or health or safety hazards. We will inform our customers of the environmental impacts of our products or services and try to correct unsafe use.

7. Environmental restoration

We will promptly and responsibly correct conditions we have caused that endanger health, safety, or the environment. To the extent feasible, we will redress injuries we have caused to persons or damage we have caused to the environment and will restore the environment.

8. Informing the public

We will inform in a timely manner everyone who may be affected by conditions caused by our company that might endanger health, safety, or the environment. We will regularly seek advice and counsel through dialogue with persons in communities near our facilities. We will not take any action against employees for reporting dangerous incidents or conditions to management or to appropriate authorities.

9. Management commitment

We will implement these Principles and sustain a process that ensures that the board of directors and chief executive officer are fully informed about pertinent environmental issues and are fully responsible for environmental policy. In selecting our board of directors, we will consider demonstrated environmental commitment as a factor.

10. Audits and reports

We will conduct an annual self-evaluation of our progress in implementing these Principles. We will support the timely creation of generally accepted environmental audit procedures. We will annually complete the CERES Report, which will be made available to the public.

These Principles establish an environmental ethic with criteria by which investors and others can assess the environmental performance of companies. Companies that endorse these Principles pledge to go voluntarily beyond the requirements of the law. The terms "may" and "might" in Principles 1 and 8 are not meant to encompass every imaginable consequence, no matter how remote. Rather, these Principles obligate endorsers to behave as prudent persons who are not governed by conflicting interests and who possess a strong commitment to environmental excellence and to human health and safety. These Principles are not intended to create new legal liabilities, expand existing rights or obligations, waive legal defenses, or otherwise affect the legal position of any endorsing company, and are not intended to be used against an endorser in any legal proceeding for any purpose.

THE CLEAN CLOTHES CAMPAIGN CODE FOR LABOR PRACTICES

The Clean Clothes Campaign is dedicated to advancing the interests of workers in the apparel and sportswear industry and the concerns of consumers who purchase products made and sold by this industry. The Campaign seeks an end to the oppression, exploitation and abuse of workers in this industry, most of whom are women. The Campaign also seeks to provide consumers with accurate information concerning the working conditions under which the apparel and sports wear they purchase are made. The Clean Clothes Campaign seeks to achieve its aims through a variety of means including a code of labor practice that would be adopted and implemented by companies, industry associations, and employer organizations. The code, which is a concise statement of minimum standards with respect to labor practices, is meant to be accompanied by a commitment by the companies adopting it to take positive actions in applying it. Companies are expected to insist on compliance with the code by any of their contractors, subcontractors, suppliers and licensees organizing production that would fall under the scope of the code.

Employment is freely chosen.

There shall be no use of forced, including bonded or prison, labor (ILO Conventions 29 and 105). Nor shall workers be required to lodge "deposits" or their identity papers with their employer.

There is no discrimination in employment.

Equality of opportunity and treatment regardless of race, color, sex, religion, political opinion, nationality, social origin, or other distinguishing characteristic shall be provided (ILO Conventions 100 and 111).

Child labor is not used.

There shall be no use of child labor. Only workers above the age of 15 years or above the compulsory school-leaving age shall be engaged (ILO Convention 138). Adequate transitional economic assistance and appropriate educational opportunities shall be provided to any replaced child workers.

Freedom of association and the right to collective bargaining are respected.

The right of all workers to form and join trade unions and to bargain collectively shall be recognized (ILO Conventions 87 and 98). Workers' representatives shall not be the subject of discrimination and shall have access to all workplaces necessary to enable them to carry out their representation functions (ILO Convention 135 and Recommendation 143). Employers shall adopt a positive approach towards the activities of trade unions and an open attitude towards their organizational activities.

Living wages are paid.

Wages and benefits paid for a standard working week shall meet at least legal or industry minimum standards and always be sufficient to meet basic needs of workers and their families and to provide some discretionary income.

Deductions from wages for disciplinary measures shall not be permitted nor shall any deductions from wages not provided for by national law be permitted without the expressed permission of the worker concerned. All workers shall be provided with written and understandable information about the conditions in respect of wages before they enter employment and of the particulars of their wages for the pay period concerned each time that they are paid.

Hours of work are not excessive.

Hours of work shall comply with applicable laws and industry standards. In any event, workers shall not on a regular basis be required to work in excess of 48 hours per week and shall be provided with at least one day off for every 7 day period. Overtime shall be voluntary, shall not exceed 12 hours per week, shall not be demanded on a regular basis and shall always be compensated at a premium rate.

Working conditions are decent.

A safe and hygienic working environment shall be provided, and best occupational health and safety practice shall be promoted, bearing in mind the prevailing knowledge of the industry and of any specific hazards. Physical abuse, threats of physical abuse, unusual punishments or discipline, sexual and other harassment, and intimidation by the employer is strictly prohibited.

The employment relationship is established.

Obligations to employees under labor or social security laws and regulations arising from the regular employment relationship shall not be avoided through the use of labor-only contracting arrangements, or through apprenticeship schemes where there is no real intent to impart skills or provide regular employment. Younger workers shall be given the opportunity to participate in education and training programs.

NOTES

1 Rosen, Robert H. (2000) "What makes a globally literate leader?" *Chief Executive*, April, 46–8.

2 Lee, Louise and Bernsytein, Arron (2000) "Who said student protests don't matter?" *Business Week*, June 12, 94.

3 Coalition for Environmentally Responsible Economies. See: http://www.ceres.org

4 http://www.cleanclothes.org/codes/ccccode.htm

5 *Starbucks and Fair Trade*, in-house pamphlet available at Starbucks retail outlets.

6 Schwartz, Peter and Gibb, Blair (1999) *When Good Companies Do Bad Things*. John Wiley, New York, p. 28.

7 Kaku, Ryuzaburo (1997) "The path of kyosei." *Harvard Business Review*, July–August, 55.

8 (2001) "The Global 1000", *Business Week*, July 9, 76.
9 Reported in Gregersen, Hal B., Morrison, Allen, and Black J (1998) "Developing leaders for the global frontier", *Sloan Management Review*, Fall.

The State of the Art

Organizations face four challenges in preparing global leaders.

» First, to understand that the nature of leadership is changing because of the global environment.
» Second, the processes needed to develop global leaders need to be formalized.
» Third, the creation of a single organizational culture, worldwide, is important.
» Fourth, each organization on the global scene will need to accommodate diverse societal needs.

"The real asset value of Foster's is the knowledge of the people ... You've got to believe that unleashing knowledge at all levels is critical for the success of the business. And you need leadership skills to make that happen."

Ted Kunkel, president and CEO, Foster's Brewing Group, Australia[1]

THE FOUR CHALLENGES FACED BY ORGANIZATIONS IN PREPARING GLOBAL LEADERS

Organizations face four challenges in preparing global leaders: first, the nature of leadership is changing; second, the processes needed to develop global leadership skills within organizations have to be formalized; third, a single organizational culture, worldwide, needs to be created; and fourth, organizations face scrutiny when their pursuit of profits conflicts with societal values. These challenges will be looked at in turn.

To take the first challenge – that the nature of leadership is changing – a major theme of this book is that leadership is being conceptualized as a form of influence that each person in an organization must be able to utilize. It is an expected skill for those who will be a part of any organization, but especially for those who will work on teams, committees, and as part of an outcome related network of any kind.

With only a rare exception or two, the leadership literature, unfortunately, reinforces the idea of an heroic CEO. Typically, leaders are seen as lone, omniscient actors who mastermind the strategy, execute the detail and, much like a superhero, return to their other-worldly headquarters to plan next steps. This may also be a reflection of the leadership literature, which is mainly an American phenomenon, and the hero, an American cultural icon. There have been some significant departures from this model, however.

For many people leadership is simply based in position, for if you don't have officially sanctioned power, how can you lead? In many studies such as the one conducted for the bestseller *Built to Last*, leadership is defined as "top executive(s) who displayed high levels of persistence, overcame significant obstacles, attracted dedicated people, influenced groups of people toward the achievement of goals, and played key roles in guiding their companies through crucial episodes in their history." For the study's authors, Collins and Porras, leaders are heroes, just as they have always been.[2]

For Warren Bennis, one of the most popular leadership gurus, leadership was not explicitly defined in his book *Learning to Lead*, co-authored with Joan Goldsmith.[3] Bennis and Goldsmith simply described what leaders do as opposed to what managers do: for example, "leaders act with integrity and competence, interpret reality, explain the present and paint a picture of the future, innovate, build trust, are effective advocates for followers and care about them." As they say, "A good manager does things right. A leader does the right things."

For some people this dichotomy helps them understand how the role of managing shifts. Unfortunately, like Frederick Taylor almost a century ago, this dichotomy suggests that there are in fact two distinct people exercising two distinct responsibilities, much like the division of work into those who think and plan and those who perform the tasks. In fact, leadership is a set of influencing skills every manager must possess. So, while the act of leading is different from the act of managing, both are required of anyone seeking a position of responsibility in organizations today and it is essential for the people we are calling global leaders.

In tracking the leadership literature over the last 20 years, it is clear the concept is changing – and dramatically so. In spite of a long history of seeing leadership as a function of top management and based solely in one's position in an organization, today leadership is increasingly being viewed as a function to be exercised by virtually everyone in an organization.

As we saw earlier, ABB under former CEO Percy Barnevik was well on its way to creating this kind of environment. Barnevik reports, "There is a tremendous unused potential in our people. Our organizations ensure they only use 5 to 10% of their abilities at work ... We have to learn how to recognize and employ that untapped ability that each individual brings to work every day."[4] In this environment, leadership isn't so much a heroic act as a catalytic one – stimulating others to utilize more of their potential more often.

ABB has created a "leadership engine." As Sumantra Ghoshal and Christopher Bartlett concluded in *Individualized Corporation*, "The real requirement of success, then, was not just resources or strategic brilliance at the top of the company but a broad-based organizational capability embedded deep in the corporate ranks."[5]

It is this last point that deserves attention, since global organizations connected by a giant telecommunications based Internet to the far corners of the globe can no longer depend on a hierarchically positioned superhero. To be a global leader should not be understood as simply leading global operations. That again is to acknowledge the leadership role as the responsibility of a single leader but on a grand scale – no longer focused on a domestic workforce but a multinational one. Global leadership is correctly understood as leading in a global context. There is a big difference. The lone ranger may not be dead but is becoming overwhelmed. There is simply too much to do, not enough time to do it, and a demand for expertise that is just not available to any one person. Thus, the new leadership is an organizational capacity to draw out the necessary expertise and influence when and where it is needed. To do this, not only must there be a consciousness that each person in taking initiative will be expected to lead at appropriate moments, but that the organization must be helping each person develop the competencies to lead.

This does not mean that everyone can or will become a CEO. It does mean that at every level of personal interaction, whether individual, small group, team, committee, task force, department, division or geographic area, people must be prepared to understand when to initiate and take the lead and when to follow; how to be most effective with others and serve the organization's mission; how to focus on task, cooperating in the accomplishment of objectives and stimulating others to contribute their best. In this way, the organization is truly energized. Is this realistic? Does it sound beyond the reach of most people's experience of organizations? Perhaps, but only if we remain stuck in the belief that leadership is about a single person taking the initiative while all the rest remain passive and receive orders. That may have indeed been the case but the demands of the new global economy require new forms of leadership. The inefficiencies that the old system could accommodate are no longer possible. The view of employees as mere instruments of a manager's will are, today, a dangerous indulgence.

Toward the end of the 1990s an interesting article by Peter Block, author of *Stewardship*,[6] simply stated that now "leaders don't matter."[7] Indeed, undue reliance on one or two individuals may be organizationally inefficient as well as dangerous to individuals by really encouraging them to be dependent on others. Explaining further, Block said, "The focus on the leader is a collective escape from responsibility. A culture of accountability will come from turning our attention away from leaders and committing ourselves to creating a deeper sense of community and citizenship."[8]

Changing organizational environments are changing leadership

This emerging concept of leadership is a response to the changing nature of organizational environments. Table 6.1 summarizes the influences which have led to new organizational characteristics requiring new leadership behavior.

The second challenge is that the processes needed to develop global leadership skills within organizations need to be formalized.

"Leaders who keep learning may be the ultimate source of sustainable competitive advantage. With that understanding, many companies are investing in leadership development (programs that help key executives learn leadership skills). As early as 1993, *Business Week* estimated that $17 billion was being spent annually on helping managers develop the thought processes and company-specific skills that could enable them to move up and lead their business areas. *Training* magazine estimates that in 1998 US companies spent $60.7 billion on training.[9] But spending isn't the only commitment. World class executives are investing significant amounts of their time personally guiding and mentoring future leaders.[10] To them, leadership development is not a luxury but a strategic necessity."[11]

While Jack Welch understood intellectually the importance of a global mindset in today's organizations, when choosing his successor at General Electric, the international experience he spoke so convincingly about was clearly not considered essential.

Table 6.1 Changing organizational environments, changing leadership.

These influences on organizations	Lead to these organizational characteristics	Required leadership behavior
Complexity	Teamwork	Facilitation skills
Competitiveness	Flexibility	Responsiveness
Opportunity	Speed	Empowerment of colleagues
Accessible information and personal technologies (knowledge tools)	Responsibility	Commitments to performance standards and outcomes
Continuous change	Learning	Stimulating thinking and sharing
Thorough professional socialization	Partnership	Peer respect and accountability
Interdependencies with internal stakeholders (employees, owners, managers)	Gainsharing	Providing rewards, celebration, and recognition
Rise of organizations as the focus for our primary attachments	Community	Fun, shared experience, relationship building

Some companies design leadership training experiences and guide the development of particularly talented individuals who will hold formal positions from which to exercise leadership. For the rest of the organization, it is still advisable to offer skills training so that when the time comes to exercise leadership at the level of team, network, task force, etc., each person is equipped to do so. The distinguishing characteristic between the two types of leadership development is the focus. Formal programs focus on formal authority, strategy, and organizational issues to a much larger extent than the latter type that helps equip each individual with the skills to influence others. Meeting management, communications, self-assessment, giving and receiving feedback, and team-building are examples of the kinds of skills available to all.

THE ELEMENTS OF A COMPREHENSIVE LEADERSHIP DEVELOPMENT MODEL

The elements of a comprehensive leadership development model should include the following:

» Top management support and involvement. Exemplary global leaders should mentor at least one or two of the participants in a leadership development program.
» A concentrated session on the organization's vision, mission, and values that are deemed essential for the success of the organization.
» Team based action learning projects that give candidates practice in using their leadership skills, working with peers on real management problems.
» Performance feedback in a 360-degree manner; that is, utilizing the perspectives of all those who work with the participant.
» Personal coaching. This can be done through either an external professional or with peer coaches trained in the skills required to be effective in the role.
» Multicultural participation and a multinational setting. Participants should meet and work in various organizational and customer sites overseas.
» A personal journal or log that helps focus the participant on a development plan that can be used as the basis for discussions with the individual's coach.

To quote Hiroshi Okuda, president of the Toyota Motor Company, Japan, "I have to make quick decisions and anticipate what might happen in the future. To do that I have to listen to people."[12]

The third challenge is the creation of a single organizational culture, worldwide.

Although globalization is irreversible, uniformity is not inevitable.
Robert Salmon, vice chairman, L'Oreal, France[13]

Clearly, the easiest task in being a global organization is establishing uniform policies and practices for the execution of most organizational functions. The not-so-easily-accomplished task, however, is to adopt values, norms, expectations, and interpersonal behaviors, ranging from how one communicates with others, to how employee evaluations will occur, to employee benefits, to acceptance of, or modification of, those unique cultural practices at each site around the world.

The American Management Association International, an organization that teaches best practices in management seminars around the world, found itself during a retrenchment in the rather embarrassing situation of having a different policy for each country working out of its European office, even when the job descriptions of the affected employees were the same. Those employees having participated on virtual teams were aware of the differences that ranged from providing a week of severance pay to over a year of severance for the same job category. The only explanation was that different countries had different laws regarding how separations were to be handled. The remaining employees were all scrambling to renegotiate their terms in light of the vast differences between countries. Not only were the affected individuals further abused by the prejudicial treatment but those remaining had another reason to leave.

While it is understood that different countries will have different laws and different wage structures, there is less toleration for treating anyone in one country differently than in another. With globalization comes vast and swift information exchange, and people's expectations of non-discriminatory treatment are raised. Of course the labor force in Mexico earning $10/day is vastly different than the same company's Michigan auto workers making $144/day and that won't change for some time, but it gets harder and harder to explain the discrepancy. When Daimler-Benz took over Chrysler, it found much to its consternation that the American minority partner was making eight times more than his Daimler-Benz boss.

Each situation needs to be handled slightly differently. For example, while it is understood that in Muslim countries employees must have the ability to honor their faith which requires prayer five times a day, it may be possible to make allowances in multicultural settings for some to exercise that practice while others choose not to. Some countries may also have relaxed such practices but each organization will need to accommodate its particular employees.

Though there will be the inevitable conflicts, misunderstandings, and sacrifices to organizational efficiency and productivity, each organization must struggle with creating and supporting a culture that everyone, everywhere in the organization can feel proud to be a member of.

CORPORATE CULTURE

Corporate culture is the social manifestation of the organization's learning and experience. It is the particular pattern of norms, beliefs, assumptions, relationships, shared meaning, and symbols that distinguish the organization's members from others. In its entirety it is a way of being and a reflection of the productive capacity of the organization's human system.

Rensis Likert, in 1961, may have been the first to identify management systems that were a precursor to the concept of culture – a broader, more comprehensive concept.[14] He confined his focus to distinct systems that result from the particular application of managerial variables such as leadership, communications processes, goal setting, and decision making in an organizational context.

With the publication of Deal and Kennedy's *Corporate Cultures: The Rites and Rituals of Corporate Life*[15] attention was drawn to aspects of organizational life that were previously ignored. They looked at rites, rituals, values, and heroes, for example, as keys to understanding not only what is important to members of an organization but also the kinds of influences that drive their current behavior. Of course those influences include management's behavior but there are many more. This led to an examination of the impact of culture on change efforts and suggested the importance of understanding the underlying cultural terrain before making any effort to change an organization.

Effective global leadership requires the careful building of a corporate culture that unifies the employees but does not conflict with local cultural sensibilities. When Wal-Mart ventured into Germany in the late 1990s it found the company cheer (give me a W, give me an A . . .) to use at motivational meetings was acceptable, as improbable as that may sound. However, the idea of having greeters who immediately welcome shoppers upon arrival or at any time they come within 10 feet of an employee in the store was not acceptable. Yet, sufficient transferability of major core values do translate and a visit to a Wal-Mart no matter where it is located will indeed result in the same look and feel as in its home US State of Arkansas.[16]

Gillette, producer of personal care and stationery products, has been a global company for almost 100 years. With 62 manufacturing facilities and 75% of its workforce of over 40,000 people overseas, maintaining the corporate culture yet guiding its evolution as the world changes is an important aspect of top management's responsibilities.

To read the Gillette Statement of Values, as any company's, you might think of it as simply a set of platitudes. If they are, then the promise of creating a high performance culture is lost. However, in Gillette's case, to cite one example, it states broad behavioral expectations in three areas: toward employees, toward customers, and corporate citizenship in the locations in which they do business. Part of the message about good corporate citizenship is its claim that "we will comply with applicable laws and regulations at all government levels wherever we do business . . . We will conserve natural resources, and we will continue to invest in a better environment."[17] In practice this might mean just respecting the law where they are, but Gillette demonstrates to its employees, customers, and suppliers alike that these statements mean something more than what they appear. Indeed, though environmental standards are lower in some of the Latin American countries in which it does business, Gillette insists that its operations conform to the higher US standard. This is how a culture is influenced by a set of value statements. But it gets there only by continually educating all employees about the meaning of the mission, vision, and values, and questioning existing behavior in light of its compatibility with the intent of the statements.

Organizational culture can be likened to a personality or to a climate, a general feeling one has when inside the organization either as an employee or a customer. It's the feel of the place. It begins with a conscious understanding of the values that are most important or, in the case of Levi Strauss the clothing manufacturer, it is a set of noble aspirations that it continually strives to realize in day-to-day behavior. Thus, once there is an understanding of what is important, it becomes necessary to help people behave accordingly. That requires significant efforts to communicate the values, establish policies and procedures that reflect the values, and reward people for exemplifying the values in practice. Thus, to ensure that the values are understood: teach. To ensure that the values are practiced: evaluate. To ensure that the values become championed by everyone: reward their manifestation.

CREATING A HIGH PERFORMANCE ORGANIZATION

Ultimately, the purpose of understanding organizational culture is to build a high performance organization – one that through its shared vision, cohesiveness, and clear strategy achieves superior results within an inherently satisfying workplace environment. Simply put: "A high performance organization sustains superior output, quality, and member satisfaction."[18]

A high performing organization is one that is productive in a high morale culture. Not all financially successful companies can be considered high performing, however. There is a free flow of information and knowledge sharing, an eye on long-term performance and a personal sense of responsibility for the performance of the whole cultivated in self-managing teams.[19]

High performance work practices are "designed to provide employees with skills, incentives, information, and decision-making responsibility that improve business performance and facilitate innovation."[20]

According to John Burdett, "High performance organizations are beginning to recognize that flat structures have inherent advantages over the traditional multi-level bureaucracies. The acronym FLAT is used to describe an organization that (1) reflects in clear, unambiguous terms the business Focus, (2) ensures that the number of Levels are congruent with effective decision making, (3) shows Alignment between the strategy, core competencies, business systems and information management, and (4) emphasizes the reality that Time is a strategic imperative. The key to organization design lies not in any single dimension but in the interrelationship of all factors."[21]

"A survey of 700 firms from all major industries found that companies utilizing a greater number of innovative human resource practices had higher annual shareholder return from 1986–91 and higher gross return on capital ... A study focusing on the *Forbes* 500 found that firms with more progressive management style, organizational structure, and reward systems had higher rates of growth in profits, sales, and earnings per share over the five-year period from 1978–83 ...

A detailed study of over 6000 work groups in 34 firms concluded that an emphasis on workplace cooperation and the involvement of employees in decision making were both positively correlated with future profitability."[22]

It may come as a surprise to some people, but "it's not the gifted individuals who make peak performance possible as much as the dynamics of belief, collaboration and support."[23] Global leaders may be forced to understand this if for no other reason than the world is too complex, distances too vast, and cultures too varied for one person, no matter how gifted, to lead in the same top-down fashion as in the fading, traditional perception of leadership.

Because high performance organizations are intense in their requirement for widespread personal participation and accountability, there is an ebb and flow of personal energy that influences the productive mood of the organization. Thus, in building a high performance organization it is also important to be on the lookout for signs of deteriorating commitment: increasing interpersonal conflicts, decreasing sense of purpose, elusive achievements, members being increasingly diverted from team business, and membership of their work teams increasing without the consent of the members. Perhaps the sure giveaway that there is trouble occurs when the term "high performance" is being used to replace "productive" or "motivated" and becomes meaningless – just another buzzword.

SEVEN THINGS CEOS NEED TO KNOW ABOUT LEADERSHIP AND ORGANIZATIONAL CULTURE

1 70% of their subordinates are afraid to speak the truth to them.[24]
2 More than 33% of their employees would leave their current jobs for a 10% salary increase or flexible work hours.[25]
3 44% of their employees would leave their positions tomorrow for more potential for advancement.[26]
4 The perception of their leadership is their most important asset and its effect is greatest among those farthest from them in the organization.
5 CEOs cannot ever know all they need to know or be all they need to be.

6 Their most important task may be to show the way to the future and engage every employee's desire to go there with them.

7 Employees should be able to answer the following 12 questions in the affirmative to verify that a positive performance culture exists:

I know what is expected of me at work.

I have the materials and equipment I need to do my work right.

At work I have the opportunity to do what I do best every day.

In the past seven days, I have received recognition or praise for doing good work.

My supervisor, or someone at work, seems to care about me as a person.

There is someone at work who encourages my development.

In the last six months, someone at work has talked to me about my progress.

At work, my opinions seem to count.

The mission/purpose of my [organization] makes me feel my job is important.

My fellow employees are committed to doing quality work.

I have a best friend at work.

This last year I have had opportunities at work to learn and grow.

(Profits, productivity, employee retention, and customer loyalty all showed a consistent, reliable relationship with these beliefs.)[27]

The most important things a CEO does are the things most CEOs will least likely want to do! That is, build the right organizational vision, mission, culture; empower people, train, and develop everyone to take on leadership responsibilities as needed; and convey what they are doing to everyone in the organization to keep them informed.

The fourth challenge is that, in the not-too-distant future, each global organization will face the same kind of scrutiny we have seen Royal Dutch/Shell, Nike, Nestle and others face when the organization's pursuit of profits runs up against conflicting societal values.

The anti-globalization coalition of environmentalists, human rights activists, and provincial interests of various kinds will raise issues that will interfere with business as usual.

THE TRIPLE BOTTOM LINE

There is a concern that the worldwide scramble of huge global organizations should be, if not centrally regulated, required to account for themselves according to a triple bottom line. Of course, the financial bottom line will always remain an essential and unarguable accounting of an organization's economic performance. That's the first bottom line. The second is an environmental bottom line that is becoming more and more acceptable to large organizations because everyone realizes the world has a serious environmental problem.

Though there is tremendous disagreement about just what needs to be done and when, the problems are many, serious, and visible. Global organizations will be increasingly held accountable not only for the impact their production processes have on the environment, but also for the "lifetime" impact of the products they produce. Soon lifecycle responsibility will be the norm and organizations will be expected to plan for the disposal or recycling of their output just as they plan for the creation of their products.

The third and most controversial bottom line is a collection of issues loosely described as social. What is the impact of organizations when they enter countries and cultures? Can they be unobtrusive partners in a positive change process contributing to the betterment of the people affected by their presence? Will they enhance the lives of their workers? Will they be good corporate citizens and members of the community? Will workers be paid a living wage, have the right to organize, and share in the health, welfare, and retirement benefits common to workers in the developed countries?

The negative answers to these questions are what have fueled the globalization backlash. Until these questions are satisfactorily dealt with they will remain on the agenda whenever international bodies meet and whenever NGOs (non-governmental organizations) seek to focus attention to their cause.

CONCLUSION

These are the four most significant and inevitable issues facing the global organization today. And just as the Internet has spread so quickly and become an integral part of business life, so too will these issues quickly become agenda items for all organizations doing business worldwide.

NOTES

1 Rosen, Robert H. (2000) "What makes a globally literate leader?" *Chief Executive*, April, 46-8.
2 Collins, James and Porras, Jerry (1994) *Built to Last*. HarperCollins, New York.
3 Bennis, Warren and Goldsmith, Joan (1994) *Learning to Lead*. Addison-Wesley, Reading, MA.
4 Barnevik, Percy, quoted in Ghoshal, Sumantra and Bartlett, Christopher (1997) *Individualized Corporation: A Fundamentally New Approach to Management*, Harper, New York.
5 Ghoshal, Sumantra and Bartlett, Christopher (1997) *Individualized Corporation: A Fundamentally New Approach to Management*. Harper, New York.
6 Block, Peter (1993) *Stewardship*. Berrett-Koehler, San Francisco.
7 Block, Peter (1997) "Leaders don't matter." *At Work*, Nov-Dec.
8 Block, Peter (1997) "The end of leadership." *Leader to Leader*, Winter.
9 (1998) "Industry Report 1998: Training Budgets." *Training*, October, 47. See also (1999) Reingold, J., Schneider, M., and Capell, K. "Learning to lead," *Business Week*, October 18, 76.
10 Byrne, John A. (2000) "PepsiCo's new formula." *Business Week*, April 10, 172 and Stewart, T.A. (1999) "How to leave it all behind." *Fortune*, December 6, 345-8.
11 Fulmer, Robert M., Gibbs, Philip A., and Goldsmith, Marshall (2000) "Developing leaders: how winning companies keep on winning." *Sloan Management Review*, Fall.
12 Rosen, Robert H. (2000) "What makes a globally literate leader?" *Chief Executive*, April, 46-8.

13 Salmon, Robert (1996) *The Future of Management: All Roads Lead to Man*. Blackwell, Oxford, p. 82 (translated from *Tous Les Chemins Mènent À L'Homme*, 1994 Interéditions, Paris).

14 Likert, Rensis (1961) *New Patterns of Management*. McGraw-Hill, New York.

15 Deal, Terrence and Kennedy, Allan A. (1982) *Corporate Cultures: The Rites and Rituals of Corporate Life*. Addison-Wesley, Menlo Park, CA.

16 McCune, Jenny C. (1999) "Exporting corporate culture." *Management Review*, December.

17 Jones, Patricia and Kahaner, Larry (1994) *Say It and Live It: The 50 Corporate Mission Statements That Hit the Mark*. Currency/Doubleday, New York.

18 Bassin, Marc (1988) "Teamwork at General Foods: new and improved." *Personnel Journal*, May, 62.

19 Reich, Robert (1994) "Leadership and the high performance organization." *Journal for Quality and Participation*, March, 6.

20 Anonymous (1993) *High Performance Work Practices and Firm Performance*. US Department of Labor, Washington, DC.

21 Burdett, John O. (1992) "A template for organizational design." *Business Quarterly*, Summer, 35.

22 Anonymous (1993) *High Performance Work Practices and Firm Performance*. US Department of Labor, Washington, DC.

23 Bassin, Marc (1988) "Teamwork at General Foods: new and improved." *Personnel Journal*, May, 62.

24 Warren Bennis, quoted at Leaders and Scholars Conference, Los Angeles, CA, November 15, 1998.

25 New York based Gemini Consulting survey of 10,339 workers. Reported in *Global Workforce*, November 1998.

26 New York based Gemini Consulting survey of 10,339 workers. Reported in *Global Workforce*, November 1998.

27 These statements were reported as part of a Gallup study in Buckingham, Marcus and Coffman, Curt (1999) *First, Break All the Rules*. Simon and Schuster, New York.

Global Leadership in Practice

Global leadership faces many challenges and requires a diverse repertoire of skills to be effective. What does it take to succeed?

» Cross-cultural adaptation: the case of McKinsey's Rajat Gupta.
» Creating a common vision: the Nokia way.
» Semco: A Brazilian exemplar of enlightened management.
» Nestlé's Global CEO.
» The qualities of a globally literate leader.
» Preparing global leaders.
» Facing the downside of globalization: culture shock.

"From fast food to pharmaceuticals, from Brazil to Thailand, moving from the periphery into the mainstream of global competition is such a big leap that it was always led from the top. In each and every case, the emerging multinationals had leaders who drove them relentlessly up the value curve. These leaders shared two characteristics. First, their commitment to global entrepreneurialism was rooted in an unshakable belief that their company would succeed internationally. Second, as their operations expanded, they all exhibited a remarkable openness to new ideas that would facilitate internationalism – even when those ideas challenged established practice and core capabilities."

Christopher A. Bartlett and Sumantra Ghoshal[1]

A study reported in *Human Resource Management*[2] reports that there are real bottom line advantages to having a management team with global experience. Indeed, without it, it is doubtful that key executives can fully grasp the complexities of the global marketplace, cultural differences, and operational contingencies outside of the home country. Global experience is still lowest among Americans – compared to their peers in Europe and Asia; only 15% of executives in the US report having overseas experience. But a growing number of CEOs report that their foreign experience was perhaps the most important factor in their leadership development. General Motors, Avon, Ford, General Mills, Case, and Outboard Marine now demonstrate to their ambitious middle managers that a foreign assignment will be helpful.

It is apparent that the methods for managing abroad and the deep and necessary relationships needed to do business there can only be understood on site. There is no way short visits or briefings can substitute for the experience; building trust and understanding between the head office and the field requires relationship building. This is even more important when different cultures, languages, and political/historical contexts exist to exacerbate mutual comprehension.

CROSS-CULTURAL ADAPTATION: MCKINSEY'S RAJAT GUPTA[3]

Though American CEOs possess the least international experience, paradoxically, US companies seem increasingly willing to appoint foreign born managers to the top spot. Foreign born professionals have been welcome and rising to prominence in US companies. Jacques Nasser, CEO of America's fourth largest company, Ford Motor, is a prime example. His appearance before televised Congressional hearings regarding the operational failure of Firestone tires on Ford SUVs (sport utility vehicles), resulting in over 100 deaths, put him squarely in the public eye. In addition, he was featured in a company public relations advertising campaign as the spokesperson for Ford, as it tried to win back public confidence in its vehicles' roadworthiness. Indeed, his Australian accent quickly alerted the public to his national identity. But Australians, Canadians, and Britons are culturally closest to Americans and have been most welcomed into the US. They have also had the easiest adjustment. Not only is language a non-issue, but the three cultures are quite similar in individualism and power distance – two prime cultural qualities that largely influences one's performance-organization fit.

Individualism-collectivism is a scale that determines whether people are concerned mostly with taking care of themselves and their families or expect the groups they are a part of to take care of them in return for loyalty to the group. Power distance is the extent to which a culture accepts the uneven distribution of authority. High power distance is tolerance for inequality in power and low power distance is the preference for a more egalitarian structure. People from Australia, the UK, and the US all tend toward individualism and low power distance.[4]

But it is Rajat Gupta, a native of India, now in his seventh year as managing director of McKinsey and Company, the oldest management consulting company of its kind in the US and one of the largest in the world, who most dramatically demonstrates the intercultural challenges faced in a global organization by an individual from a vastly different cultural orientation. McKinsey has over 7000 consultants in 84 offices worldwide. It operates with a "one firm" policy emphasizing a common service standard for all clients. The network structure of the firm allows it to deliver its knowledge-based support services to consultants anywhere, anytime.

McKinsey has been ranked number one or two as the most desirable company to work for by graduating MBAs. It is a culture that immediately utilizes the expertise of each of its staff and encourages consultants to take a leading role in meeting customer needs. Indeed, Gupta refers to McKinsey as a "firm of leaders." As he tells it:

"... when you have a firm, which consists essentially of leaders, you must give them an enormous amount of room to exercise their leadership capabilities. It's a firm which is a very flat, horizontal structure, with a great deal of independence, and with a great deal of entrepreneurial energy in it, with an umbrella of values and just an overall understanding of this broad strategy we have. We let people take lots and lots of initiatives, in terms of what they think is right. Because it is a firm of leaders, if they more or less understand the values and the strategies of the firm, they will invariably do the right things ... We have about 80 to 100 performance cells ... They are very much autonomous and they are not organized in any hierarchy ... So all these performance units, in a theoretical sense, report to me, which means they don't report to anybody, because nobody can have 80 or 100 people reporting to them. This implies that the task of the managing partner is to create the right set of values, the right culture, and the right environment to motivate people, and let them do what they are best at. If you can give them that kind of freedom, then I think they will do extraordinary things."

Gupta points out that in an organization of leaders serving on committees, task forces, or other organizational units is a duty for everyone and that the nominal leadership roles of those groups can rotate quite freely to bring in fresh energy and a new perspective. This keeps a large number of the consultants motivated, as does striving for the position of partner. Of course McKinsey has a reputation of being an extremely challenging and demanding practice field for top flight MBAs who frequently gain enough exposure to the business world to land attractive new positions elsewhere. In that sense the McKinsey experience is considered a great training ground for other organizations. So, because of turnover and growth where 25% of the workforce is new each year, a major task of the managing director is to reinforce the organizations' vision, strategy, and values while creating opportunities, globally, for motivated individuals to achieve their career objectives.

In this environment of bright leaders the managing director needs to be in service to his or her consultants' aspirations and success. "The nature of the task," Gupta says, "is being first amongst equals: you're not anybody's boss. If you tried to do that, you would not succeed. I personally feel very much that I am there to serve; it's a servant leader kind of style. I've been elected at the pleasure of my fellow partners. I'm there to make them successful."

Rajat Gupta brings a style of leadership to McKinsey, a global consulting firm, that clearly is communicative, reflective, highly networked, and open. He sees his role as primarily a servant of the organization – a facilitator of success. How does this cooperative, facilitative style work in the highly individualistic US-based McKinsey culture? Clearly it creates a tension but one Gupta has managed well. It is his style to draw people out and help them reach their own conclusions, even when they might prefer that he simply make decisions as is customary of individuals in similar positions in other American companies. He acknowledges that it might cause frustration among his colleagues but persists nevertheless. He prefers to let decisions evolve – to "percolate" – which is a style more frequently found in Asia. Indeed "bottom-up" decision making is usually associated with Japan but is characteristic of many Asian cultures where collectivism – thinking of the welfare of the group–is the norm and consensus seeking is valued.

CREATING A COMMON VISION THE NOKIA WAY

Like Gupta's consensus seeking, Finnish Nokia spends much time in the field listening to its employees and customers before developing its plans. The vision is one that is shared, indeed instigated by people throughout the company, and much time and effort is spent getting input to insure that the vision makes sense to everyone. To develop a uniform understanding of the company's global strategic vision, meetings called the "Nokia Way" are held all over the world to brainstorm Nokia's potential and its desired future. These meetings involve people from the lower ranks throughout the company. The results of these discussions are sent to headquarters where they are synthesized into a strategic vision by the top management team, which is then transmitted back to the field in frequent and thorough presentations. Thus, a uniformity of vision is developed with the input of all of those who wish to contribute and involve participants from all aspects of the business worldwide.[5]

SEMCO: A BRAZILIAN EXEMPLAR OF ENLIGHTENED MANAGEMENT

"We don't just have philosophical discussions – we are creating a new reality."

Laura de Barros, director of human resources, Semco

Along a narrow, winding road on the outskirts of São Paulo, Brazil, there is an organization providing the latest proof that humanistic management and full worker participation is possible and profitable.

Semco, a diversified company producing unglamorous air-conditioner coils and nautical pumps, and distributing manufacturing control systems, employs about 200 people. Semco has gained recognition being the subject of another CEO confessional (*Maverick*[6]) going well beyond what we have come to expect of enlightened companies doing good.

But Semco is more than the result of a single CEO's commitment and *noblesse oblige* as seems the case with Anita Roddick's Body Shop or Tom Chappell's Tom's of Maine (a company making environmentally safe personal hygiene products without artificial ingredients). At Semco some rather unusual practices have been institutionalized, such as workers selecting their bosses. These practices cannot be unilaterally discontinued. Some of the companies that were exemplars yesterday have been subject to some dramatic reversals. For example, Ben & Jerry's Homemade before its sale to Unilever in 2000, and its absorption into a mainstream business, was touted as a model for socially responsible business that was mindful of the environment, a good corporate citizen where it conducted business, and a great place to work. Much of that has changed and the once highly regarded practice of maintaining a maximum CEO salary spread of seven times the lowest paid employee was abandoned when Ben & Jerry decided to recruit a "professional CEO."

Such practice seems unlikely at Semco, though management does maintain the sole right to strategic choices that do affect everyone. For example, a shift away from manufacturing into services cost many jobs but units were spun off and were initially supported by Semco until they successfully stabilized rather than being summarily eliminated.

While Ricardo Semler rightfully takes credit (and is given credit by Semco employees) for introducing the radical reformulation of management-labor practices at Semco and converting an authoritarian regime into a democratic one, clearly the credit for success goes to the employees, to the unions, and to the managers who, over a 12-year period, worked (and continue to work) on making the necessary commitments to the experiment. Place no pedestals under Semler or Semco. They aren't perfect and many of the practices we read about are unevenly applied, and real disparities exist between the roles of labor and management, but they are committed to closing any gap between aspiration and behavior.

The real test of any exemplar is its sticking to its principles in tough times. In the US, it is frequently said that participative management is a fair weather practice. As soon as times change, out goes democracy and top-down control returns. Watching the sad parade of layoffs again sweeping the US and the dot com meltdown demonstrates the point. At Semco, it is just the opposite. When all is smooth sailing there are fewer meetings and less of a need for group decision making. When times are tough and the strategic decisions threaten employees, meetings are held to assemble the best thinking and mutual commitment necessary to deal with the challenges. This is a sharp departure from the American practice of top-down decision making by the managerial élite under such conditions.

Freewheeling, open, fearless communication characterize meetings as the focus of everyone's attention is directed at mutual problems. Sometimes there is a standoff and discussions get bogged down. They don't always reach consensus but that isn't the point. What is important is that everyone gets a chance to make their case fully. They know that decisions need to be made and if one's approach isn't accepted now, they'll get their chance later. Everything is tentative; they proceed knowing that a decision is "the one for now." As circumstances change so, too, do the solutions. And everyone knows that. It's not about pleasing everyone all the time or about following rules or about political correctness. It is about running a business as an extension of core beliefs about life and understanding that all members of the organization are citizens entitled to responsibility and, therefore, a voice. Everyone is held accountable for their actions.

It was remarkable hearing of Semco's belief that it is management's job to help everyone realize their innate power. It is remarkable because of the long history of authoritarianism and paternalism in Brazil's government, corporate world, unions, and families. To break from that tradition took courage and conviction but it worked because of one immutable fact – organizations can select and terminate their members. If people cannot or do not want to exercise their potential and take responsibility, Semco is a miserable place in which to work. Part of the pain over the last 18 years of creating their brand of workplace democracy was having to sort out those who were willing to embrace the new culture and those who could not. Though this turnabout sounds like a massive change, it really wasn't. It was about "being" and, therefore, defining one's values in order to determine if the new emphasis on democracy would reflect who people are. Ultimately Semco struggled with developing new ways of expressing its values and inventing new structures and policies to make that happen. In demonstrating its care for each person in the process, and respecting the fact that finding a fit is a mutual exercise, the sorting process enabled each person, as well as the company, to determine if they shared the same values and goals.

In discussions with John Mills, a British expatriate in charge of sales, Marcio Batoni, director of Semco Johnson Controls, and Laura de Barros, director of human resources, the most striking impression was their enthusiastic and spontaneous candor. Each in turn reiterated the imperfections in the Semco system and the need to try hard to make their beliefs work. It isn't about techniques. It isn't about profit. It is about living a way of life that, as only one of its virtues, is profitable.

The Semco story illustrates three major points. First, change is possible and large-scale change may require a long-term, ongoing process of reinforcement and adjustment. Second, when alignment of individuals' values and organizational practices occur, powerful synergies are created. Third, and this is vital for global leaders to understand, culture is dynamic and can therefore be changed. Semco provides the most dramatic example of a conversion to corporate democracy in the last 30 years. And the example came to us not from Europe or the US, but from one of the most hierarchical, authoritarian, and stratified cultures in the world.

It should come as no surprise to anyone who has been part of a successful change effort to learn that change is a process not an event. As such, in a multicultural setting it is important to build in time for adjustment, for understanding, and for personal enquiry in order to assure that everyone has an opportunity to be heard and an opportunity to accommodate the new demands and expectations arising out of the change effort.

SEMCO'S VALUES

Semco held five years of monthly meetings discussing people's beliefs and how to practice them in the workplace. They were guided by several principles:

» power is already inside people . . . we need to let it out;
» people have the right to be different;
» begin to understand how to work with one another by first understanding people's values and aspirations;
» align beliefs with organizational practices;
» give those who want to learn, an opportunity to do so;
» give all a chance for self-determination – choice; and
» don't over plan – go with needs as they are discovered.

NESTLÉ'S GLOBAL CEO

Nestlé, based in Vevey, Switzerland, is a far-flung food company most noted for its chocolate, milk, and coffee products, and has over 200,000 employees in factories in almost 80 countries who produce almost $50 billion in sales annually. Though the 160-year-old company has been an international enterprise for almost its entire history, it is only recently that Nestlé could be characterized as truly a global company.

In the 1970s, Nestlé was thought to be an exploitive MNC selling infant formula to third world countries mostly in Africa and Asia by way of a marketing program to dissuade mothers there from breast feeding their children. But the relatively expensive formula was diluted by mothers and mixed with contaminated water, ultimately leading to malnutrition and the death of their infants. Taking a posture typical among many corporations toward its critics, who accused Nestlé of ignoring the plight of these women and children, Nestlé in turn accused the concerned interest groups of being anti-capitalist communists. Only after an effort to boycott Nestlé did a serious dialogue begin.

Today, Peter Brabeck-Letmathe, Nestlé's current CEO, is a tangible symbol of how Nestlé has evolved. A native of Austria, his first language is German but he is fluent in French, Italian, Portuguese, and English, and speaks Spanish at home with his Chilean wife and their two grown children. He worked in Chile, Venezuela, and Ecuador prior to becoming CEO.[7] Some of Nestlé's 8000 brands are sold in every country of the world and Brabeck-Letmathe is given credit for taking the old company "run as a collection of fiefdoms" and turning them "into an effective single global company."[8] Where competitors like Coca-Cola and Kellogg are struggling, Nestlé has increased margins by almost a third, realized cost savings through some consolidations without labor unrest, and expanded some key segments through successful acquisitions. Much of this can be attributed to a functional understanding of intercultural operations that serves as the basis of Nestlé's global presence.

QUALITIES OF A GLOBALLY LITERATE LEADER

Robert Rosen identified four "literacies" that constitute an effective global leader: personal literacy (understanding and valuing yourself); social literacy (engaging and challenging others); business literacy (focusing and mobilizing your organization); and cultural literacy (valuing and leveraging cultural differences).[9]

PREPARING GLOBAL LEADERS

Black and Gregersen remind us that "the primary objective of global leadership training is stretching someone's mind past narrow domestic borders and creating a mental map of the entire world."[10] They report how a Korean MNC, Sunkyong, draws participants in their global leadership development program and assigns them action learning projects. For one group, their task was to spend time in China studying liquid natural gas opportunities and a potential partner recommended by the government. The result of their program not only helped develop leadership skills and broaden their experience in a multicultural setting, but also, because the project was real, the results were beneficial to the company. The team recommended not partnering with the initial candidate because they determined they needed capabilities unavailable in that company. This kind of conscious global training with a real impact on an organization's performance enables individuals to broaden their perspective and create new mental models of the world.

The case of TRW

TRW consciously trains leaders for global operations and includes both formal training as well as career assignments that will help test the individual in the field. Their Management Resource Review Process (MRRP) attempts to identify promising candidates for senior level career tracks that prepare individuals for promotion who continue to develop the requisite global leadership skills.[11]

Like Sunkyong, TRW establishes multicultural business teams to help participants build personal networks and grasp the breadth of resources available to them worldwide. The teams share best practices and each participant has the opportunity to see what works and what doesn't in various parts of the company and in various regions of the world. These structured experiences also enable the participants to work together to solve real issues they face. With the participation of senior management they are not only able to address immediate concerns but also develop a uniform understanding of the vision of the company and how global operations can best manifest the vision.

Several key aspects of TRW's strategy and vision are included in the structured program with the participation of senior management. Included in the curriculum are topics such as global strategy, leadership style and behavior, culture, and organizational capabilities. There are also discussions with top management including the CEO about the current state of the business.

The global leadership program consists of several pedagogical methods that utilize both classroom and field work. Participants look closely at their own behavior and work on real problems. Modules are two weeks long and between modules, participants are expected to work on individual and group projects. Because there is personal reflection on individual behavior, group work, access to senior management, and a team-based structure that draws from an intercultural set of participants, individuals begin to view managerial responsibilities through a new global lens. And as Neary and O'Grady report, at the final presentations, participants would discuss "... lessons learned, rather than a list of formal recommendations. The priority was the learning involved, rather than a focus on implementation of the project statements."[12]

To further reinforce the emphasis on learning, personal learning agendas are created by each participant and one-on-one coaching is provided to help each person meet his or her specific developmental goals.

LESSONS FROM THE TRW GLOBAL LEADERSHIP DEVELOPMENT PROGRAM[13]

» Involve senior management in all aspects of the program and include them in a formal coaching or mentoring role with program participants whenever possible.
» Assign small teams for more focused learning.
» Arrange local on-site support but avoid "catering" to all the participants' needs. Let them take the initiative in arranging program activities, field work logistics, and team meetings.
» Facilitate the development of each participant's and team's specific and focused action learning project and development agenda.
» Ensure that all projects are meaningful and relevant to their learning and work performance.
» Create continuity between training groups.

> » Encourage "alumni" activities and help establish an ongoing peer support group of graduates.

Matsushita (building relationships with their customers and society)

A unique business philosophy propelled one of Japan's leading industrialists to create one of the world's largest corporations whose primary purpose is "to create peace and prosperity throughout the land."[14] Konosuke Matsushita was only 22 when he started his company to mass produce an electric socket that he invented. Soon he was producing insulating plates, flashlights, adapter plugs, wiring fixtures, radios, batteries, and sundry other electrical appliances. Today it is the world's number one consumer electronics maker, with brands such as National, Technics, Panasonic, JVC, and Quasar, with 335 operating units in 45 countries.[15] Sales of $58 billion place it at number 26 on *Fortune* magazine's list of the world's largest corporations.[16]

Matsushita's mission statement was formulated in 1929: "Recognizing our responsibilities as industrialists, we will devote ourselves to the progress and development of society and the well-being of people through our business activities, thereby enhancing the quality of life throughout the world."

MATSUSHITA'S SEVEN GUIDING PRINCIPLES

"Every company, no matter how small, ought to have clear cut goals apart from the pursuit of profit, purposes that justify its existence among us."

Konosuke Matsushita

By August, 1937 the company developed the following seven-point code to guide its activities and provide each of its employees (today, almost 300,000 people) with a collective sense of purpose:

1. National service through industry

We will contribute to the progress and welfare of the community and nation.

2. Fairness

Without this spirit no one can win respect nor can be respected no matter how wise or capable they may be.

3. Harmony

We shall work together as a family in mutual trust and responsibility.

4. Struggle for betterment

It shall be our policy to encourage trust and self-reliance that each may gain self-respect through his or her own endeavor and struggle hard for betterment.

5. Courtesy and humility

We shall respect the rights of others. We shall be cordial and modest. We shall praise and encourage freely.

6. Adjustment and assimilation

As the world moves forward we must keep in step.

7. Gratitude

We shall repay the kindness of our associates, our community, our nation, and our foreign friends with gratitude.

BEING AN INSTRUMENT OF CHANGE

There are a number of ways in which an individual can use himself or herself as an instrument of change. Here are two to consider:

"1 Changing others. Holding a personal vision or desire, backed by sufficient personal energy, one may, through the uses of power and persuasion, succeed in changing a targeted system, situation or even culture ... That might mean you would assess the people you work with to determine who has that combination of desire and energy, and if your views are compatible, using your energy and skills to support that thrust.

2 Changing self. By developing a sufficiently open mind that is willing to extend and expand its perspectives, one may discover aspects of an existing system, situation or culture that were not previously recognized ... That might mean spending time understanding and appreciating the existing system/culture so that change efforts will be limited and elegant – sufficient to achieve a well focused purpose and considerate of those with significant stakes in the outcome, but not an importation of some currently popular Grand Plan."[17]

THE DOWNSIDE OF GLOBALIZATION: CULTURE SHOCK

Not everyone will succeed in a cross-cultural experience. In fact, it costs upward of $250,000 per failure for a key manager sent abroad who cannot adjust. It is not unusual that because of exemplary technical skills an individual will be sent overseas to bail out a subsidiary, be the HQ person on the spot, or be thought to be a perfect fit for the problems faced at the overseas site. Unfortunately, even astronomical "expat" packages to entice a skilled person to accept an international posting cannot guarantee that the individual will succeed. There is the very stark reality that an overseas posting often results in an individual or a family member falling victim to "culture shock" and needing early repatriation.

Culture shock is the disorientation that occurs in an individual, resulting in that person's inability to function in a new cultural environment. This occurs when one's own frame of reference is so fixed that differences can not be tolerated. It also occurs when the familiar manner of navigating the social landscape becomes inappropriate or ineffectual in a new cultural setting. Mild stress accompanies all immersions in a different culture until it becomes thoroughly familiar and one is able to function independently and fluidly in it.

Humans are by nature sensors and organizers of stimuli; when stimuli do not fit into a familiar pattern, a "shock" might result. To deal with this shock and to master the new environment, two preliminary steps are necessary.

First, the individual must identify which of his or her usual behavior patterns are totally unacceptable in the new environment and begin to change them if possible. At the very least the expression of unacceptable behaviors must be controlled to suit the new context. Second, individuals must attempt to desensitize themselves and accept many of the differences they encounter as legitimate. This is achieved by consciously, deliberately, disengaging from the impulse to summarily judge, dismiss or ignore one's new circumstances.

Of course this is easy to say and tough to do. Frequently our disorientation occurs subconsciously and we may be unaware of its impact. What one is not aware of one cannot handle, because what is not seen is thought not to exist. Hence, awareness programs that deliberately expose one to other cultures, belief systems, and behaviors in the home country are a first step to charting the challenges ahead. They are not, however, a substitute for the ability to engage with people in the new environment and to be able to discuss one's experience there.

It is important that while one is adjusting, he or she must accomplish the difficult task of communicating respect, a healthy curiosity of others, a non-judgmental attitude, empathy, personal flexibility, and a tolerance for ambiguity. Paradoxically, possession of this ability would mitigate culture shock itself and if one is able to demonstrate these qualities at the outset, the shock will indeed be minimal.

However, there is a problem that confounds our global leaders and it is that in being accommodating and adaptable, they must not lose sight of their purpose – to get results, to be effective in achieving the organization's goals. Rather than fearing being awkward or making devastating *faux pas* by living a prescriptive set of behaviors people need to remember to be themselves. Remember, there are two factors that help you succeed.

First, because much of the world is headed toward an industrial and perhaps even a post-industrial way of life, one can expect a generally cooperative appreciation of the need to achieve the organizational goals of efficiency and effectiveness. As an Indian expatriate professor in Singapore, Anant Negandhi, concluded a long time ago, ". . . we do not contend that the studies in cross-cultural management are obsolete, but we do feel the logic of technology is taking over man's differing beliefs and value orientations. Increasingly, the road is becoming one."[18] In a very real sense the trauma of a confrontation between an industrial era mindset and a pre-industrial era mindset is becoming rarer and rarer, and reducing the degree of disorientation that managers feel when dealing with newly emerging economies.

Second, people in virtually every culture are willing to give a visitor the benefit of the doubt while he or she is adjusting and learning appropriate behavior. In effect, where there is goodwill, all parties to the intercultural experience can be stretched a little to accept others' differences. The basis for a strong common bond exists when people have to rely on each other and they share the same understanding of the purposes of their organization – the same corporate vision, identity, performance standards, and organizational culture.

THE CULTURAL MANAGEMENT MATRIX

So, is there a way of navigating differences as they relate to getting the job done that is respectful? The answer is "Yes." For novices, heading overseas, it will be useful to employ the culture management matrix. This is a tool that helps individuals identify likely organizationally relevant behavioral consequences of particular cultural characteristics.

The purpose of the matrix is threefold. First, it is an attempt to facilitate the effective management of people by individuals assigned to overseas operations. Second, by focusing on culturally rooted behavior, it helps the manager avoid destructive conflicts, misunderstandings, and disruptions due to the clash of differing assumptions, expectations, and demands between foreign national and local. Third, in a general sense, it is a quick way to help the manager reduce the extent of any culture shock.

The central element of the culture management matrix is the identification of the actual behavioral expression of underlying cultural values, beliefs, and attitudes found in the work setting in the new cultural environment.

TIPS

Do guard against transpersonal invalidation, wherein one individual attempts to deny (invalidate) the experience of another person. For example it is common in Bali to set aside an offering to the spirits. This is as true for large businesses as small village homes and shops. To call the practice silly or not to honor its tradition would be insensitive and offensive. In a multitude of often very subtle ways, we find ourselves judging the experience of others and thus run the risk of not only misunderstanding but of insulting others.

Second, **do** guard against projective cognitive similarity, which leads us to believe that simply because others share experiences with us or look like us or hold some of the same beliefs as we do, they are fundamentally just like us; that their values and behaviors will be predictable and like our own. The Japanese, for example, have become very "Westernized" in dress, work organization, and material lifestyle. Yet the Japanese are extraordinarily different from Westerners and this is demonstrated in almost every facet of life. As just one example, the idea of the group is fundamental to Japanese people who derive a great deal of their identity through their association with others, from the school they attended, the company they work for, or the nation as a whole. While team work and patriotism characterize Western behavior as well, those behaviors are more transient in service to individual gain – especially so in Anglo countries.

Third, **do** know yourself well enough to clearly establish a sense of how far you are willing to be stretched without inappropriately compromising your own fundamental beliefs and ways of behaving (unless of course they are totally unacceptable in the new environment).

If people had the ability to quickly change their predispositions to better suit the needs of the new environment, they would not suffer during the adjustment period. But humans, alas, are not so versatile. Hence the culture management matrix may help one understand the challenge to be faced. Coping and adjustment strategies should also be developed and they become more important as the differences between the guest and the host diverge. Sometimes the challenge is simply too great to master and the person assigned overseas risks failure, early repatriation, or massive stress.

In creating the culture management matrix focus on the following six areas:

1 a general managerial function or goal;
2 an assessment of expected behavior: home country ideal;
3 host culture characteristics;
4 observed behavior (manifestation of the characteristics);
5 consequences of violating host culture practice; and
6 prescription (notes and comments).

Each of the six areas will now be examined using the example of a non-Japanese person working in Japan.

1. A general managerial function or goal: leadership

Consider what this means to you and how your philosophy of leadership influences your behavior. For example, is leadership something that only one person, usually the formal boss, does? For the sake of our example of a non-Japanese working in Japan let us say he or she also arrives with the traditional notion of leadership, that the manager in charge takes the initiative to frame issues, generate some strategies, and allocates resources reflecting his choice of next steps and so on.

2. An assessment of expected behavior – home country ideal: what techniques of leadership do you use?

If you believe leadership rests with an individual boss would your technique of leadership be a directive decision making process where you dispense with consultative meetings and make decisions unilaterally? To continue with our Japanese example, we can generalize about what we see but be cautious about stereotyping. The Japanese seem to be very group oriented and individuals are pressured to place group performance above their own interests. It isn't unusual for quality circles for example or other group experiences to find an extraordinary interest among individuals to be active contributors in service of the group.

3. Host culture characteristics: what is the idea of leadership in the host culture?

What philosophy of leadership seems to apply? And where is leadership centered? In observing groups and people in relationships there is often a great deal of silence as the subtleties of place in the group and consensus building require much personal consideration and reflection as well as group discussion. Being part of a group in Japan means few physical barriers, much interaction between people, and relationship building and maintenance even after normal work hours.

4. Observed behavior (manifestation of the characteristics): how is leadership exercised?

For example, what techniques of decision making are used? Though there is a hierarchy one observes it is usually smaller than in a similar concern in the West. At one point Toyota had 5 layers of hierarchy when General Motors had 12. You might not see the anxiety Japanese people feel about inclusion or exclusion in a group but it is at the core of the national psyche. Thus, behavior that can be interpreted as isolating an individual can create an existential crisis.

5. Consequences of violating host culture practice

Since people don't usually prefer to work in isolation or strictly speaking in obvious competition with others, not enhancing group identity through shared experiences of belonging and appreciation of each person's role in the group, motivation and morale would collapse and interpersonal tension would result.

6. Prescription (notes and comments)

In our example of a decisive, individualistic manager from the West working in Japan, we can see that a sensitivity to a group orientation will be required. This will necessitate some personal, conscious effort to be more inclusive and to work more as part of a group. The idea of bottom-up decision making is real. It means that work groups are seen as most expert in their area of responsibility and because of the belief in continuous improvement, it is the individual's job to wholeheartedly support the betterment of their work. This frequently results in the creation of a "ringi," a document proposing a significant new idea to be considered by successive relevant individuals until a consensus is developed. In this way, people contribute their thinking to the betterment of the collective work and help move the process along toward a decision.

KEY LESSONS

Since global leadership skills are not instinctive but learned, expose participants to development programs that include intercultural experience at home and abroad.

It is important to broaden one's perspective to accept differences. Remember that there are many different ways of accomplishing basically the same thing. This principle of "equifinality" helps us understand that different practices in different cultures aren't necessary wrong but just another way of doing something.

It is possible to prepare to work through differences in a conscious fashion to gain some control over the experience. The culture management matrix helps one do this.

NOTES

1 Bartlett, Christopher A. and Ghoshal, Sumantra (2000) "Going global: lessons from late movers." *Harvard Business Review*, March–April, 141.
2 Carpenter, Mason A., Sanders, Wm. Gerard, and Gregersen, Hal B. (2000) "International assignment experience at the top can make a bottom-line difference." *Human Resource Management*, Summer/Fall, 227–85.
3 Based on an interview in *The Academy of Management Executive*, May 21, 2001, 31–44.
4 First introduced to the comparative management literature in (1984) Hofstede, Geert, *Culture's Consequences.* Sage Publications, Thousand Oaks, CA.
5 Fox, Justin (2000) "Nokia's secret code." *Fortune*, May 1.
6 Semler, Ricardo (1993) *Maverick: The Success Story Behind the World's Most Unusual Workplace.* Warner, New York.

7 Data from Bradshaw, Thornton and Vogel, David (1981) *Corporations and Their Critics*, McGraw-Hill, New York and Rossant, John (2001) "The stars of Europe," *Business Week*, June 11, 67–82.

8 According to Morgan Stanley Dean Witter's London analyst Sylvain Massot, quoted in Rossant, John (2001) "The stars of Europe," *Business Week*, June 11, 78.

9 Rosen, Robert H. (2000) "What makes a globally literate leader?" *Chief Executive*, April, 46–8.

10 Black, Stewart J. and Gregersen, Hal B. (2000) "High impact training: forging leaders for the global frontier." *Human Resource Management*, Summer/Fall, 173–84.

11 Neary, D. Bradford and O'Grady, Don A. (2000) "The role of training in developing global leaders: a case study at TRW Inc." *Human Resource Management*, Summer/Fall, 185–93.

12 Ibid., 189.

13 Adapted from Neary and O'Grady, ibid.

14 Matsushita, Konosuke (1984) *Not For Bread Alone: A Business Ethos, A Management Ethic.* PHP Institute, Kyoto, Japan.

15 http://www.hoovers.com/co/capsule/3/0,2163,41873,00.html

16 Kahn, Jeremy (2001) "The world's largest corporations." *Fortune*, July 23.

17 Herman, Stan, author of *Authentic Management* quoted from *ODNet Listserv*, November 12, 1998.

18 Negandhi, Anant (1983) "Management in the Third World." *Asia Pacific Journal of Management*, **1** (No. 1).

Key Concepts and Thinkers

This chapter provides an overview of the major thinkers and key concepts in the field of global leadership.

» A glossary of global leadership terms and concepts.
» A descriptive list of major thinkers to the field.

"When people walk in the door, they want to know: What do you expect out of me? What's in this deal for me? What do I have to do to get ahead? Where do I go in this organization to get justice if I'm not treated appropriately? They want to know how they're doing. They want some feedback. And they want to know that what they're doing is important."

Fred Smith, founder and CEO, Federal Express[1]

CONCEPTS

Arenas of leadership

Leadership is practiced in a variety of arenas and will, accordingly, take various forms. Within each of the following main arenas, the focus and practice of leadership will be distinct.

Intrapersonal

The intrapersonal arena involves leadership of oneself. It is establishing one's values, understanding one's motives, and learning skills that will aid in self-assessment and self-control.

Interpersonal

The interpersonal arena involves the leadership of another person. Here one learns how to engage with others and build strong positive relationships. Typically, this is a one-on-one process that results in understanding how we influence others and how we are influenced by others.

Team

The team arena involves leading a small number of people toward a mutual objective. More than simply the sum of the individual relationships, in this arena we learn how to generate team enthusiasm, cooperation, and performance, while maintaining positive performance expectations of one another and remaining satisfied at being a part of the team. Here we may first get exposure to the issues surrounding leadership at a distance – especially for global leaders and if members are located at remote distances necessitating a telecommunications mediated relationship.

Organizational

Leading in this arena involves leading at a distance. Though many of the people one will lead are in the same physical location such as a company headquarters, they are subject to influence but not face-to-face. In this case a person may be simply a floor above or a continent away. But it is the distance and the difficulties of knowing the indirect impact of one's influence that remains the challenge in this arena.

Societal

Leading in this arena involves an understanding of the role and impact of decisions on the larger community – no matter where it is in the world. Indeed, today it is quite common for actions in one place (selling infant formula in Africa) to have a profound impact elsewhere (stimulating a boycott in North America because of the way the infant formula is being marketed).

Change

What is change?

Ultimately, leadership is about change. To influence another person or a group of people – even to influence oneself – is to seek change.

But for many managers, dealing with change is a source of pain and failure both personally and organizationally because change is often erroneously thought of as an event, and not as a dynamic process. Perhaps that is another quality that distinguishes managers from leaders.

The attempt at control and the imposition of a manager's will, quite paradoxically, almost always results in failure and delay; precisely the opposite of what one would expect. After all, aren't managers paid to be decisive, make changes, and know how to utilize their human resources? Aren't managers paid to cause change, not react to change? Yet, the act of trying to control a change process is much like trying to control the spill of a water glass on a dinner table. The chaos that results is much like the confusion that sets in when change is simply announced in organizations by a manager who is a position holder and not a genuine leader. For the global leader, managing change will be an essential component of his or her agenda.

Change: the case of the missing battery

In an effort to develop a "customer connection initiative," GTE Mobilnet (now Verizon) set up a task force to determine exactly how it could become tops in customer service. One of the team members, Ben Powell, learned that just because people say they want something doesn't mean they'll like it if they get it. "We got all their [employees'] comments and listened to their questions, and we really tried hard to address their concerns," he says. "But when we went back and explained how things were going to change, they stared at us like, 'What have you done?' We sure didn't get any standing ovations."

In late summer of 1993, for example, Powell and his teammates began trying to persuade staffers at Mobilnet's 350 service centers around the US to send new phones out the door with batteries already in them. "Instead of saying to the customer, 'Here's your phone, go home and charge it for eight hours before you use it,' the salespeople were really happy to be able to promise a phone that worked right away," Powell says. But the idea was a tougher sell for the service folks who had to install the batteries: "We've had to overcome their objections one by one, piece by piece, bit by bit."

Here's what the team said, repeated, with variations, about 350 times: "You can't see why you need to be bothered with this? Here are sales figures showing how much revenue we lose by making customers wait to use the phone. The average customer, like the kid with a new toy, calls everybody he knows from Boston to Baton Rouge when he first gets the thing, but only if it has a charged battery in it. Don't have room to stock all those extra batteries? We'll help you redesign your workspace to accommodate them. Can't predict how many of which battery you'll need on hand at any given time? We'll provide data to help you with those projections, and teach you how to use them. Can't afford any of this to come out of your operating budget? We'll find it for you."

"When you meet this kind of resistance, the only thing you can do is just keep plugging away at it until there are no more excuses," says Powell, sounding tired, "and, after a year and a half, we're really just getting there now." Powell and his crew rely on sheer doggedness to make change stick.[2]

This account of a seemingly simple change initiative is instructive in many ways. It illustrates some of the essential issues leaders must face in all change programs. The first element is the individual who must implement the change. The technicians found an endless number of objections to putting batteries in the cell phones and never acted as if they understood the reasoning at all; though to an observer, the purpose is patently obvious.

The formal leader or position holder, in solving a problem, creates a problem for the targets of the change effort by requiring them to alter routines and be disturbed from a static state to a state of flux.

But more is going on here. Intelligent people dragging their feet on something so apparently inconsequential tells us that they did not "own" the overall mission of the customer connection initiative. They weren't involved in examining the problems with customer service, and probably weren't consulted about customer service, much less rewarded for it. Finally, they weren't given any options in instituting the new phone assembly process. Perhaps worst of all, it doesn't appear that they were kept very well informed about the need to make the changes in the first place. The task force was created at corporate level and driven by its own findings. The "leader" was attempting to impose a solution on people who didn't perceive they had a problem.

This case is also instructive in pointing out that while there was an insufficient communication effort and information was slow in getting to the people who needed it most, work processes were being altered on a piecemeal basis that could actually interfere with the overall telephone assembly and shipment process. The size and weight of the battery would alter shipping costs, packaging, warranty fulfillment, and a variety of other steps in the customer service process that begins right at the point of manufacture.

Given the circumstances surrounding the customer connection initiative we see that change wasn't an isolated event but rather the culmination of a lengthy decision making process apparently introduced with the first effort to improve customer service. You could actually say it began much earlier, perhaps with the rather modest standing of the product in the marketplace or as feedback accumulated in the marketing department regarding the product's appeal, perhaps even in the billing department with the recognition of the product's lower than normal usage. The point is that decisions made anywhere in a rather long line of events result in distant traumas as change events affect increasing numbers of people in the organization. An intervention at any point in the potential chain of events discloses a leader's value set.

Change management

There isn't any fool-proof methodology that can guarantee the smooth, unobstructed implementation of the change in this case. No matter what one does there will always be a period of time required to adjust. There will always be a period of time required to plan, communicate, involve, discuss, and act to reshape a process in a new direction, or to change one person's or a group's behavior. In other words, there is always an effect when a formal leader acts. We can, however, increase our ability to plan for the impact of our actions on others and the system.

Change as a process

If we continue to see change as a thing or event – something out there that we must learn to respond to – we will forever be a victim of circumstances and nothing will alter that fact. When we see change as the process of life itself, and all that we do within our organizations, we can then begin to lead and manage it as the embodiment of our sense of purpose and organizational vision. Then change becomes a welcomed and powerful personal and organizational force for the achievement of our collective objectives.

Had the people in Mobilnet's customer service center understood this and how their roles were vital to the success of the corporate vision, the "change" program might have been accomplished faster. Had they been readied for a flexible response and had the confidence that their issues would be dealt with to make the program successful, they would likely have embraced rather than resisted "change."

Of course getting there is to understand some emerging truths: that to manage is to work with others as part of a network of resources and the organization is everyone in it – not just a few at the top or a "steering committee." Remember, in the old world of work, it may have been possible to simply order compliance and spend the bulk of one's time as a manager supervising and cajoling people to perform as required. That world is fading fast. There is no time for that anymore. Nor is it the most effective way to lead. And, of course, it is not very satisfying for anyone involved. For the global leader with the added burden of distance from the point of change, this is more important to understand and appreciate.

REASONS FOR RESISTANCE TO CHANGE

» The purpose of the change is not made clear.
» People affected by the change are not involved.
» Existing group habits are ignored.
» People may experience a fear of failure.
» There is poor communication regarding the change.
» Existing group habits are ignored.
» The appeal for change is for one's personal advantage.
» The change creates excessive work pressure.
» Job security may be threatened.
» The personal cost is too high or the rewards inadequate.
» There is a lack of trust or respect in the initiator.
» Change is too rapid or too much is required immediately.
» People are satisfied with the status quo.
» Past experience with change efforts have been negative.
» There is an honest difference of opinion.

GAINING SUPPORT FOR CHANGE

» Encourage participation of those affected by change in task forces, teams, action research, and feedback.
» Help the subjects experience the need for change.
» Show success.
» Maintain open and frequent communication; explain what people should expect and give the rationale.
» Avoid a we/they mentality; encourage identification with the results of change.
» Satisfy the needs and allay the fears of those affected by the change.
» Encourage voluntary constructive change; establish a climate of innovation and reward change.

Culture shock

Culture shock is the disorientation that occurs in an individual, resulting in that person's inability to function in a new cultural environment. This occurs when one's own frame of reference is so fixed that differences cannot be tolerated. It also occurs when the familiar manner of navigating the social landscape becomes inappropriate or ineffectual in a new cultural setting. Mild stress accompanies all immersions in a different culture until it becomes thoroughly familiar and one is able to function independently and fluidly in it. But with culture shock one is overwhelmed by the stress in the new environment and immobilized.

Emotional intelligence

Emotional intelligence (EI) consists of the personal capabilities involved in controlling one's behavior and relationships. It is comprised of five components first articulated as EI by Daniel Goleman in 1998.

1 **Self-awareness**: the ability to recognize and understand your moods, emotions and drives, as well as their effect on others.
2 **Self-regulation**: the ability to control or redirect disruptive impulses and moods; the propensity to suspend judgment – to think before acting.
3 **Motivation**: a passion to work for reasons that go beyond money or status; a propensity to pursue goals with energy and persistence.
4 **Empathy**: the ability to understand the emotional makeup of other people; skill in treating people according to their emotional reactions.
5 **Social skill**: proficiency in managing relationships and building networks; an ability to find common ground and build rapport.[3]

Clearly these qualities are differentiated from IQ – one's intelligence particularly in manipulating data, analytical skill, and other technical aspects of acquiring and using knowledge. The qualities meant by EI are that "certain something" we recognize in the charismatic, the extrovert, the eager network builder, and initiator of relationships. It is this particular set of qualities that, according to Goleman and others' research, account for leadership effectiveness.

Global leadership

Global leadership will involve developing an international perspective for building relationships, creating strategy and executing plans across borders, cultures, and vast distances in a 24 time-zone marketplace that cannot be achieved without varied international experience. Global leadership requires an active sensitivity to fundamental differences among people that impact the success of influence attempts. It also means having a global framework that informs one's thinking about all aspects of the organization and the people who constitute its essence. The main aspect of global leadership that differentiates it from one's personal experience of leadership in the home culture is the absolute necessity to deal with people of other cultures as colleagues and peers. And, in virtually every country in the world, working with colleagues means working with groups of people, teams, and networks.

Global organization

A global organization conceptualizes the earth as a single venue in which to assemble and utilize resources in its productive effort. The MNC is now morphing into a new entity, which not only does business overseas but also defines itself more as a global, rather than national, citizen. Clearly MNCs are no longer national instruments. Rather, they are an independent collection of vast commercial interests that operate completely on the world stage. While in their infancy during the cold war, MNCs operated from a central hub with field personnel sent by and managed from the home office. Today, operations are entirely dispersed and constitute an earth-straddling network of resources connected by a proprietary Internet (or intranet) with satellite and cellphone-mediated voice and video communications, featuring e-mail, instant messaging and access to all required real time data. Cheap labor, proximity to physical resources, and cheap transportation costs have created a world sourcing challenge to minimize costs, maximize reach to customers, and reduce the time needed to connect the knowledge of needs with their fulfillment anywhere in the world.

Globalization

According to Thomas L. Friedman,[4] "The driving idea behind global-ization is free market capitalism – the more you let market forces rule and the more you open your economy to free trade and competition, the more efficient and flourishing your economy will be. Globalization means the spread of free market capitalism to virtually every country in the world. Globalization also has its own set of economic rules – rules that revolve around opening, deregulating and privatizing your economy." And the practical impact of this is the creation of a world culture that threatens to destabilize governments, local cultures, and aspirations.

Groupware and networks

Given the inevitability of the telecommunications and knowledge revolution and its influence on the workplace, new methods of communicating and decision making are needed. This becomes apparent as computerization of functions, telecommuting, and interpersonal long-distance networking become commonplace – especially in global organizations. Groupware is a term representing any computer application that facilitates interpersonal communication, decision making, and scheduling or event coordination.

These programs allow two or more people either at one site or distant from each other to communicate, share information and jointly work on the same databases, issues, documents. The World Wide Web is enabling organizations to link employees everywhere for the purpose of real-time communications and for instantaneous information flow and exchange.

The use for communications and even the high-tech capabilities of sending and receiving all types of data still, however, does not overcome the fundamental inhibitors of useful, meaningful, fearless communications. The technology does not replace the need to learn how to communicate, to trust those you communicate with, and to be trustworthy to others. Though companies often spend small (and large) fortunes to create these systems, they frequently find they have neglected the underlying basis for the success of their communications processes.

Leadership

Leadership is as much about how work gets done as it is about what gets done and who does it. Leadership is clearly being recognized as a widespread social phenomenon necessary for the achievement of a group's collective objectives and not just an expression of a position in a hierarchy or a chain of command. Thus, we define leadership as a form of influence and a type of interaction between an initiator and a follower. Leadership is a set of initiatives and responses between people for the purpose of achieving mutual objectives intended to result in collective effectiveness and personal enrichment over time.

Leadership development

Leadership development is the formal or informal deliberate improvement of an individual's capacity to influence others for the purpose of achieving mutual objectives intended to result in collective effectiveness and personal enrichment over time.

Learning organization

A learning organization is an adaptive enterprise that acquires and applies new knowledge. It encourages and supports employees' efforts to develop their individual capacities and share knowledge with one another. It is ultimately a cooperative, creative, and innovative workplace.

Brian Dumaine was one of the first to identify the concept. He called it "A consummately adaptive enterprise with workers freed to think for themselves, to identify problems and opportunities, and to go after them."[5] But it is more than that. The learning must become part of the organizational mind; it must be accessible to others. Furthermore, according to David Garvin, "A learning organization is defined as an organization skilled at creating, acquiring and transferring knowledge, and at modifying its behavior to reflect new knowledge and insights."[6] Personal qualities needed to work well in a learning organization include having an ability to learn, probably having some higher education experience, and the ability to solve problems and work without supervision with good interpersonal skills.[7]

Motorola reports: "We used to hire people because they could manipulate parts, they could put things together with their hands ... Now we really need the whole worker. You have to have somebody to do simple programming, read, write commands, interpret information on terminals, and do preventive maintenance."[8]

"Eight specific factors influence an organization's capacity for learning. These are: (1) the extent to which an élite group or single point of view dominates decision making; (2) the extent to which employees are encouraged to challenge the status quo; (3) the induction and socialization of newcomers; (4) the extent to which external data on performance, quality, consumer satisfaction, and competitiveness are cultivated or suppressed; (5) the equity of the reward system and distribution of status and privilege; (6) the degree of empowerment of employees at all levels; (7) the historical legacy and folklore; and (8) the integrity of contention management processes – particularly with respect to surfacing hard truths and confronting reality."[9]

There are barriers and limitations preventing organizations from becoming learning enterprises. Peter Senge[10] outlines several organizational learning disabilities that inhibit the organization's capacity for learning, as follows.

1 Believing that "I am my position." This limits your consciousness and motivation to a specific job description by seeing yourself merely as a particular profession or set of skills. Thus, individuals do not see the organization's performance as their responsibility and become disassociated from it.

2 "The enemy is out there." For any mistake there is a convenient villain who can be blamed. This prevents enquiry, openness, and dialogue – and particularly systems thinking.

3 "The illusion of taking charge." Doing something and asserting responsibility to solve problems (address issues/events) demonstrates our competence and position.

4 "The fixation on events." Because every event is believed to have a cause and since we have a position and are supposed to know what is happening, we must take responsibility to determine the explanation of events. It results in very short-term, particularistic decisions and a very limited understanding of the whole. Life is seen as a series of events rather than an unfolding of a process.

5 By focusing on events we are blind to processes. Because incremental changes are not perceived as important their accumulation goes unnoticed until it is effectively too late. We must resist the temptation to neglect the long-term implications of current conditions, as innocuous as they may appear in the present.

6 "The delusion of learning from experience ... We learn best from experience but we never directly experience the consequences of many of our most important decisions ... and the analysis of the most important problems in a company, the complex issues that cross functional lines, becomes a perilous or nonexistent exercise." In short, it is possible that 20 years of experience is a single year repeated 20 times.

7 "The myth of the management team." Because of norms and pressures and the idea of keeping appearances, hard decisions and dissenting voices are not heard. Too often they are lost in the need to maintain a "united front," or to "pull together," or to "go along with the prevailing wisdom" and to "be professional." Thus, the so-called team discussion is merely an exercise in group think.

Confronting these collective learning disabilities is vital. It is necessary to develop a safe environment where fearless communication and a questioning attitude are not only possible but essential to uncover weaknesses in current positions and to unlock the group's potential.

Mindset

Mindset describes the distinctive viewpoints, needs, and agendas that determine how an individual views and engages categories of events at work.[11] Similar to mental models (below), the two terms are frequently used interchangeably. The primary difference appears to be that a mindset may be conscious as well as deeply ingrained thereby being an element of our motives. That is we "see what we want to see."

Mental models

Mental models are deeply ingrained assumptions, generalizations, or even pictures or images that influence how we understand the world and how we take action.[12] These models diverge within cultures and even more so between cultures. An understanding of our and others' assumptions, generalizations, and values help us to understand how we formulate our beliefs and our consequent behavior when we undertake to lead (influence) others.

Mentoring/coaching

As teams become a larger part of workplace life and as the pressure to learn and experiment increases, leaders play more of a developmental role than ever before. Instead of being expected to know everything and to "boss" people, managers are becoming more like team players and coaches. For global leaders it is that much more important. This requires encouraging and teaching, more than giving orders. Accordingly, a manager's goals are developmental as well as control oriented. The purpose here is to help each team member, or subordinate, perform their best, and learn how to improve.

"Coaching focuses on discovering actions that enable and empower people to contribute more fully, productively, and with less alienation than the control model [the traditional management model] entails."[13]

It is an attractive basis for a relationship because "People have more respect for a coach than they do for any other authority figure."[14]

Mentoring has another meaning usually involving the furtherance of a protégé's career and giving guidance about the company and the nether regions out of reach of the protégé. More broadly it is the development of a personal relationship with an older or more experienced individual who takes an interest in a younger person's development in its many aspects, not just organizationally.

There are several qualities of successful mentors, which include (1) personal commitment; (2) respect for individuals and for their abilities and their right to make their own choices; (3) ability to listen and to accept different points of view; (4) ability to empathize with another person's struggles; (5) ability to see solutions and opportunities as well as barriers; and (6) flexibility and openness.[15]

"Coaching is that conversation which creates a new management culture, and is not a technique within the old culture."[16] A coach sees possibilities that you cannot. They may not be better performers but, as observers, are able to see opportunities and flaws that individuals may not. They help you see yourself afresh – and honestly – either measured against an ideal or against your own potential.

Those who go to a coach generally are open to improvement, eager to learn from mistakes, and willing to try a new approach. People do not normally try to "look good" for a coach, or to convince him or her of how much they know, or what fine performers they already are.

Contrast this with the way people commonly relate to a manager. Most often they hide or justify mistakes, attempt to "look good," and listen defensively rather than openly.[17]

According to Evered and Selman, essential elements of coaching include the following:

1 partnership, mutuality, relationship;
2 commitment to producing a result and enacting a vision;
3 compassion, generosity, non-judgmental acceptance, love;
4 speaking and listening for action;
5 responsiveness of the player to the coach's interpretation;
6 honoring the uniqueness of each player, relationship, and situation;
7 practice and preparation;
8 willingness to coach and to be coached;
9 sensitivity to "team" as well as to individuals; and
10 willingness to go beyond what's already been achieved.

Furthermore, much like in a high performing organization or learning organization, they claim that "creating an organizational culture of and for coaching" requires an organization to:

1 educate people in the parameters of effective coaching;
2 commit to undertake a specific project with a specific timetable;
3 determine the "players" in the project;
4 declare who will be the coach in each project relationship and what the person or persons being coached is/are committed to accomplishing;
5 be prepared for "breakdowns" as the project progresses;
6 allow the day-to-day actions of the project to emerge from openings (new possibilities) that occur naturally in conversations with a coach;
7 validate and acknowledge accomplishments and breakdowns as opportunities to regenerate the originating commitment to the project; and
8 complete everything as the players go along.

Multinational corporation

According to the United Nations in 1975 there were 7000 transnational corporations; in 1994 there were 37,000.[18] And that figure is rapidly increasing. The transnational business is simply one with a business presence in more than one country. Though the organization has operations, investments, or marketing representatives in another country, if it does not think of the earth as contiguous with its sourcing for product, personnel, and all aspects of the production and delivery process, it is not a global organization in the fullest sense.

Organizational culture/corporate culture

Organizational/corporate culture is the social manifestation of the organization's learning experience. It is the particular pattern of norms, beliefs, assumptions, relationships, shared meaning, and symbols that distinguish the organization's members from others. In its entirety it is a way of being and a reflection of the productive capacity of the organization's human system. Similar to an individual's personality, each organizational culture is unique.

Practice field

A practice field is any situation in which an individual, team, or organization deliberately sets out to apply new behavior. Sometimes it occurs in an offline training environment, simulation, or test market. Sometimes it is in real time where the emphasis isn't so much on "practice" as it is on knowingly undertaking something new in the spirit of learning and improving based on feedback from the event.

Transpersonal invalidation

Transpersonal invalidation is the act of invalidating another person or persons; making them wrong in a subjective way, denying their experience and/or dismissing them based on a power advantage and not an objective or rational basis.

While this is a fundamental cause of interpersonal conflict that is demonstrated frequently in the workplace, individuals prone to behave this way are likely to do so more frequently when confronted with people from other cultures or, indeed, when first working overseas. This practice may be a symptom of culture shock as well as a form of intolerance, disrespect, or an inability to manage interpersonal relationships.

Triple bottom line

The triple bottom line was popularized by John Elkington who defined it as an organization being accountable for its financial performance, its environmental impact, and its social mindfulness. While economic performance has long been dissected in infinitesimal ways, the environmental impact of an organization has only recently been evaluated and usually in a superficial manner. Social accounting is virtually non-existent unless a blatant disregard for the law has occurred. The triple bottom line is, however, the subject of growing interest, especially in light of the anti-globalization backlash.

Virtual team

Typically, a global organization will utilize virtual teams to conduct much of its business. At the very least a network of individuals will be assembled from around the world to work together on a specific problem and then disband. These teams will frequently assemble and disband as the needs of the organization requires.

THINKERS

Warren Bennis

Warren Bennis is university professor and distinguished professor of business administration at the Marshall School of Business, University of Southern California. He is also a visiting professor of leadership at the University of Exeter (UK). He is one of the most prolific writers on leadership and has published 27 books on leadership, change, and social systems. His most recent book is *Managing the Dream*.

Bennis is a humanist in the traditional sense of the word. He is an advocate of personal adaptation, of continuous personal and organizational learning, experimentation and understanding how to create meaning as a motivator of human behavior. Leaders must take the responsibility because they are in a position that demands that they take responsibility. By the same token, they can't do it all so they need to develop a leadership team and develop leadership throughout the ranks to build a successful organization.

Compaq fired its CEO, according to Bennis, because "he didn't want to listen to the bad news. And that is the most common reason why CEOs fail. They just do not pay attention, they don't have peripheral vision. They can't see the inflection points that are going to influence and affect their business, whether it's demographic, regulatory, technological or fashion."[19]

Being adaptive and open is even more important globally simply because the territory is so big and competitors and innovations can emerge from anywhere. Between learning and adapting a leader must become extremely flexible to succeed today.

Perhaps Bennis's most familiar work is *On Becoming A Leader*, which focused on how people become leaders. "They range all over the map in background, experience, and vocation," Bennis reported of his subjects, "but they have in common a passion for the promises of life and the ability to express themselves fully and freely . . . full, free self-expression is the essence of leadership."[20] It is to this point that he was to comment at a 1998 seminar when he said that "70% of executives do **not** speak the truth to power." Perhaps this is one of those defining qualities that establish credibility and integrity and separate the real leaders from something else, perhaps a brand X type of leadership that is less than what it can be. This is no small point. In an era where layoffs, downsizings, and the social contract seems to be torn asunder once again, people in organizations are desperately in need of a social environment in which they feel they can focus on the task at hand, trust that their interests will be a legitimate part of the interests of the organization and that they can speak the truth.

So, for Bennis, one of the essential ingredients to achieving leadership as well as succeeding at it is a high degree of confidence in oneself and the ability to communicate fearlessly.

Another essential is focus, a point he comes back to in many of his writings and one he illustrated with a dramatic and oft quoted story about Karl Wallenda, an aerialist. In 1978, while walking a 75-foot high wire in downtown San Juan, Karl fell to his death. In recounting the tragedy, his wife, also an aerialist, remembered that all he talked about for three months before attempting this feat, was falling. He had never discussed falling before; he always focused on making it.

Bennis found in his interviews for *Leaders* that ". . . when Karl Wallenda [or anyone] poured his energies into **not falling** rather than walking the tightrope, he was virtually destined to fail." (Emphasis in the original.) Focus on achieving one's goals propels one further and on a course likely to succeed more often than focusing on not failing.

Bennis's work has consistently been positive, insightful, humanistic – and a must read.

Highlights

Bennis, Warren (2001) *Managing the Dream: Reflections on Leadership and Change*. Perseus Books, New York.

Bennis, Warren (1994) *On Becoming A Leader*. Addison-Wesley, Reading, MA.

Bennis, Warren and Goldsmith, Joan (1994) *Learning to Lead: A Workbook On Becoming A Leader*. Addison-Wesley, Reading, MA.

Bennis, Warren and Nanus, Burt (1985) *Leaders: The Strategies for Taking Charge*. Perennial Library, New York.

Bennis, Warren, Parikh, Jagdish, and Lessem, Ronnie (1996) *Beyond Leadership: Balancing Economic, Ethics and Ecology*. Blackwell, Oxford.

Bennis, Warren, Spreitzer, Gretchen, and Cummings, Thomas G. (eds) (2000) *The Future of Leadership: Today's Top Leadership Thinkers Speak to Tomorrow's Leaders*. John Wiley, New York.

Heenan, David A. and Bennis, Warren (1999) *Co-Leaders: The Power of Great Partnerships*. Wiley, New York.

Philip R. Harris and Robert T. Moran

There was a time in the late 1970s and early 1980s when Harris and Moran were the only ones writing about the practical applications of cross-cultural research. Their books were the first to demonstrate the ways to succeed overseas and how to think through the interpersonal behaviors that impact one's own behavior.

With sections on leadership in globalization, communications, negotiations, and change, they survey the arenas of leadership in which one is likely to confront challenges. In addition they set out a good portion of their most recent edition of *Managing Cultural Differences* to discuss how to do business with major cultural groups around the world, including often ignored Africa.

Over the last 20 years they have come to edit a series of books that are written for the global leader. Most have voluminous illustrations of their points and mini-cases as well as hands-on guidelines and in some cases a step-by-step guide to applying their concepts.

They are the series editors for the *Managing Cultural Differences* series published by Gulf Publishing, now part of Butterworth-Heinemann.

Highlights

Elashmawi, Farid and Harris, Philip R. (1993) *Multicultural Management: New Skills for Global Success.* Gulf Publishing, Houston, TX.

Harris, Philip R. and Moran, Robert T. (2001) *Managing Cultural Differences: Leadership Strategies for a New World of Business*, 5th edn. Butterworth-Heinemann, Woburn, MA.

Simons, George F., Vásquez, Carmen, and Harris, Philip R. (1993) *Transcultural Leadership.* Gulf Publishing, Houston, TX.

John P. Kotter

John Kotter has been known as an expert on change management and leadership for over 20 years. He holds the Matsushita professorship of leadership at Harvard University and has written an interesting though non-critical book of his benefactor.

Matsushita Leadership, as the book claims, describes Matsushita's accomplishments as a leader, author, educator, philanthropist, and management innovator, which "are astonishing, and outshine even Soichiro Honda, J.C. Penney, Sam Walton, and Henry Ford." In this immensely readable book, Kotter relates how Matsushita "created a large business, invented management practices that are increasingly being used today, helped lead his country's economic miracle after World War II, wrote dozens of books in his latter years, founded a graduate school of leadership, created Japan's version of a Nobel Prize, and gave away hundreds of millions to good causes."

Though Kotter became somewhat more adoring than dispassionate with his review of Matsushita's life and impact on Japan (and the world), he does speak of the tremendous achievements of a man who began life with none of the usual advantages, none of the usual dreams and accomplishments that we usually associate with great success. Indeed, the entrepreneur's mind and energy sustained him when his organization grew into a multinational spanning the globe. He was able to make the transition from single product innovator to chairman of a globe girdling enterprise that became the largest manufacturer of consumer electronics. Most remarkably he did so while advocating, actually preaching, the idea that leadership was not only a means to a productive end for organizations but a social responsibility.

Perhaps Kotter's most enduring contribution is to have brought the Matsushita lessons to the English speaking world – and they are considerable and worth studying.

From a technical perspective, perhaps his most important contribution was the "eight stage process of creating major change."

For Kotter, a leader who, by definition, is a change agent, creates change by: "1 establishing a sense of urgency; 2 creating the guiding coalition; 3 developing a vision and strategy; 4 communicating the change vision; 5 empowering broad based action; 6 generating short term wins; 7 consolidating gains and producing more change; and 8 anchoring new approaches in the culture."[21]

Highlights

Kotter, John P. (1999) *John P. Kotter on What Leaders Really Do*. Harvard Business School Press, Cambridge, MA.

Kotter, John P. (1997) *Matsushita Leadership: Lessons From the 20th Century's Most Remarkable Entrepreneur*. Free Press, New York.

Kotter, John P. (1996) *Leading Change*. Harvard Business School Press, Cambridge, MA.

Robert Rosen

Robert Rosen is assistant clinical professor of psychiatry at the George Washington University School of Medicine. He is also president and CEO of the non-profit Healthy Companies Institute in Washington, DC, which was created by a MacArthur Foundation grant.

As Max DePree, retired chairman and CEO of Herman Miller said, "Healthy companies [are] about shared ideals, shared goals, shared respect, and a shared sense of values and mission." Rosen's first book, in 1991, set out to describe several strategies for building healthy companies. For Rosen, writing in *The Healthy Company: Eight Strategies to Develop People, Productivity and Profits*, a healthy company is characterized by several key values: 1 a firm belief in decency; 2 a commitment to self-knowledge and personal development; 3 respect for individual differences; 4 a spirit of partnership; 5 a high priority for health and well being; 6 appreciation for flexibility and resilience; and 7 a passion for products and processes. Naturally he acknowledges that healthy people make healthy organizations and healthy organizations make healthy profits.

The biggest lessons: first, select people who have these values; and second, be sure the organization builds processes and practices to live these values. Unfortunately, organizations hire simply to fill positions and not necessarily to create a healthy company.

His second book was *Leading People: The Eight Proven Principles for Success in Business*. They are: 1 creating a vision; 2 building trust; 3 encouraging participation; 4 lifelong learning; 5 utilizing the power of diversity; 6 encouraging creativity; 7 having integrity; and 8 building community.

In both of these books, the reader is given a tour inside some of the most remarkable companies to meet leaders who make these principles come alive. *Leading People* uses mini-cases of over 30 people who exemplify his principles and show how they each bring out the best. For example, we meet Alan Mulally, senior vice president of airplane development at Boeing, who exemplified creating a participative environment in building the Boeing 777. "7000 people, in over a dozen countries working in 238 separate design teams, spent four years and $4 billion to create the 777. The plane ... has 3 million parts, from 1500 suppliers located in 62 countries worldwide." That is a global leadership challenge of enormous proportions. And it was executed within budget and on time.

Perhaps the case of Alan Mulally inspired Rosen to look more closely at global leadership. His most recent book is *Global Literacies: Lessons on Business Leadership and National Cultures*. This work surveyed over 1000 senior executives, interviewed 78 CEOs of firms in 28 countries, and categorized his successful leadership into four distinct groups of competencies: personal literacy (understanding and valuing yourself); social literacy (engaging and challenging others); business literacy (focusing and mobilizing your organization); and cultural literacy (leveraging culture for competitive advantage).

According to Rosen, "My recent research shows that valuing multi-cultural experience and developing leadership at all levels of an organization are the two best predictors of success in the global marketplace."

Highlights

Rosen, Robert H. (with Patricia Digh, Marshall Singer, and Carl Phillips) (2000) *Global Literacies: Lessons On Business Leadership and National Culture*. Simon & Schuster, New York.

Rosen, Robert H. (with Paul Brown) (1996) *Leading People: The Eight Proven Principles for Success in Business*. Penguin Books, New York.

Rosen, Robert H. (with Lisa Berger) (1991) *The Healthy Company: Eight Strategies to Develop People, Productivity, and Profits*. Jeremy P. Tarcher, Los Angeles, CA.

Website: www.healthycompanies.com

Peter Senge

Peter Senge has been speaking about the systems nature of organizational behavior since the publication of his first book, and bestseller, *The Fifth Discipline: The Art and Practice of the Learning Organization*. In that book he clearly laid out the five tasks of a leader in creating the environment conducive for learning. Clearly leadership at all levels needs a command of the five disciplines: 1 an understanding of systems thinking (seeing the whole and its dynamics); 2 the habit of personal mastery (clarifying and deepening one's personal vision and devotion to self-improvement); 3 understanding one's own and others' mental models and their influence on behavior (the ingrained assumptions and inferences we hold about reality); 4 an ability to build a shared vision (binding people together around a common identity and sense of destiny – the essence of leadership); and 5 understanding how to develop team learning (using dialogue to help team members think together).

His second book, written with a team of colleagues from his consulting company, Innovation Associates (since merged with Arthur D. Little Consulting), put the principles to work. *The Fifth Discipline Fieldbook* gives readers concrete methods for creating learning organizations. One of the most dramatic insights in the *Fieldbook* that demonstrate how our mental models stimulate specific behavior that in turn reinforces our mental models is their Ladder of Inference.

It works like this:

» Step one: "I select data from what I observe." This is influenced by how you perceive and your motives. Much of this is unconscious, a product of habits, biases, training.
» Step two: "I add meanings (both cultural and personal)." Here is where the inference process really begins.
» Step three: "I make assumptions based on the meanings I added."
» Step four: "I draw conclusions."
» Step five: "I adopt beliefs about the world." At this point you reinforce the meanings you attributed to the initial data you selected![22]

This is one of many tools available for personal, group and organizational development.

Highlights

Senge, Peter M., Kleiner, Art, Roberts, Charlotte *et al.* (1999) *The Dance of Change: The Challenges to Sustaining Momentum in Learning Organizations*. Currency/Doubleday, New York.

Senge, Peter M., Ross, Richard, Smith, Bryan *et al.* (1994) *The Fifth Discipline Fieldbook: Strategies and Tools for Building a Learning Organization*. Currency/Doubleday, New York.

Senge, Peter, M. (1990) *The Fifth Discipline: The Art and Practice of the Learning Organization*. Currency/Doubleday, New York.

NOTES

1 Fishman, Charles (2001) "Fred Smith." *Fast Company*, June, 66.
2 Fisher, Anne B. (1995) "Making Change Stick." *Fortune*, April 17, 121–9.
3 Goleman, Daniel (1998) "What Makes A Leader." *Harvard Business Review*, November–December, 95.
4 Friedman, Thomas L. (1999) *The Lexus and the Olive Tree: Understanding Globalization*. Farrar Straus Giroux, New York, p. 8.

5 Dumaine, Brian (1989) "What the Leaders of Tomorrow See." *Fortune*, July 3, 48.

6 Garvin, David A. (1994) "Building a Learning Organization." *Business Credit*, January, 19.

7 Barrow, M.J. and Laughlin, H.M. (1992) "Toward a Learning Organization 1: The Rationale." *Industrial and Commercial Training*, 24 (Issue 1), 3.

8 Alster, Norm (1989) "What Flexible Workers Can Do." *Fortune*, February 13, 63.

9 Pascale, Richard Tanner (1991) *Managing on the Edge*. Touchstone, New York, p. 236.

10 Senge, Peter (1990) *The Fifth Discipline*. Currency/Doubleday, New York.

11 Culbertson, Samuel A. (1996) *Mind-Set Management: The Heart of Leadership*. Oxford University Press, New York, p. 330.

12 Senge, Peter (1990) *The Fifth Discipline*. Currency/Doubleday, New York, p. 8.

13 Evered, Roger and Selman, James C. (1989) "Coaching and the Art of Management." *Organizational Dynamics*, Fall, p. 16.

14 Andrew DuBrin, professor of management, Rochester Institute of Technology.

15 Internal Memorandum, DEC Corp., Maynard, MA.

16 Evered, Roger and Selman, James C. (1989) "Coaching and the Art of Management." *Organizational Dynamics*, Fall, p. 16.

17 Ibid.

18 Schwartz, Peter and Gibb, Blair (1999) *When Good Companies Do Bad Things*. John Wiley, New York, p. 3.

19 Bernhut, Stephen (2001) "Managing the Dream: Warren Bennis on Leadership." *Ivey Business Journal*, May, p. 36.

20 Bennis, Warren (1994) *On Becoming A Leader*. Addison-Wesley, Reading, MA, p. 2.

21 Kotter, John P. (1996) *Leading Change*. Harvard Business School Press, Cambridge, MA, p. 21.

22 See Senge, Peter M. *et al.* (1994) *The Fifth Discipline Fieldbook: Strategies and Tools for Building a Learning Organization*, Currency/Doubleday, New York, p. 242, for a discussion of the Ladder of Inference and how to apply it to explaining your behavior.

Resources

This chapter gives you immediate access to some of the best resources available worldwide to further your understanding of all aspects of global leadership.

» A sample of associations that focus on leadership and management from a behavioral perspective are included.
» A short bibliography that represents the major concepts outlined in this book is included.
» A sampling of English language magazines and journals from around the world is included to give you a range of perspectives on the many aspects of global leadership and a feel for what is available to you globally.

"If there is technological advance without social advance, there is almost automatically, an increase in human misery."

Michael Harrington

ASSOCIATIONS

A sampling of English speaking associations in Asia, Europe, and North America of importance to global leaders

The Aspen Institute

1333 New Hampshire Ave., NW, Suite 1070
Washington, DC 20036
T(202) 736 5800
F(202) 467 0790

The Aspen Institute is an international nonprofit educational institution dedicated to enhancing the quality of leadership through informed dialogue. It convenes men and women who represent diverse viewpoints and backgrounds from business, labor, government, the professions, the arts, and the nonprofit sector to relate timeless ideas and values to the foremost challenges facing societies, organizations, and individuals.

http://www.aspeninst.org

Academy of Management

c/o Pace University
PO Box 3020
Briarcliff Manor, NY 10510–8020
T(914) 923 2607
F(914) 923 2615

Divisions and Interest Groups: Business Policy & Strategy, Careers, Conflict Management, Entrepreneurship, Health Care Administration, Human Resource Management, Gender and Diversity in Organizations, International Management, Management Education & Development, Management History, Managerial Consultation, Managerial & Organizational Cognition, Operations Management, Organization Development & Change, Organization & Management Theory, Organizational Behavior, Organizational Communication & Information

Systems, Organizations & the Natural Environment, Public & Non-Profit Sector Research Methods, Social Issues in Management, Technology & Innovation Management.

http://www.aom.pace.edu

American Productivity and Quality Center

123 North Post Oak Lane
3rd Floor
Houston, TX 77024–7797
T(800) 776 9676
T(713) 685 7260
F(713) 681 0367

The American Productivity and Quality Center (APQC) helps enterprises manage change, improve processes, leverage knowledge, and increase performance by becoming more agile, creative, and competitive. These pursuits require high-quality information, strategies, skills, knowledge, experience, contacts, and best practices. APQC provides access to best practices, research services, benchmarking studies, networking, education programs, publications, events and more – enabling companies to break out of conventional thinking and excel with best practices.

http://www.apqc.org/

American Psychological Association

750 First Street, NE
Washington, DC 20002
T(202) 336 5500

The American Psychological Association (APA) is the largest scientific and professional organization representing psychology in the US and is the world's largest association of psychologists. Through its divisions in 50 sub-fields of psychology and affiliations with 59 state, territorial, and Canadian Provincial associations, APA works to advance psychology as a science, as a profession, and as a means of promoting human welfare by the encouragement of psychology in all its branches in the broadest and most liberal manner.

http://www.apa.org/

American Society for Training and Development

1640 King Street, Box 1443
Alexandria, Virginia, 2313–2043
T(703) 683 8100
T(800) 628 2783
F(703) 683 1523

Vision: A world-wide leader in workplace learning and performance.

Mission: We provide leadership to individuals, organizations, and society to achieve work-related competence, performance, and fulfillment.

Strategic Directions: Engage and partner with all members and customers to understand their needs and expectations and respond with value-added solutions to strengthen learning and performance in the workplace.

http://www.astd.org

Ashridge Management College

Ashridge, Berkhamsted
Hertfordshire HP4 1NS UK
T(44) 1442 841000
F(44) 1442 841036

Independent center for management and organization development. Mainly UK based business, but increasingly international both in public and tailored offerings.

http://www.ashridge.org.uk

Association for Quality and Participation

801-B W 8th Street
Cincinnati, OH 45203–1607
T(800) 733 3310
F(513) 381 0070

AQP serves as an advocate and learning resource for individuals, teams, organizations, and communities to design, implement, and sustain quality and participation practices for high performance.

http://www.aqp.org/

Association for Management Education and Development

14–15 Belgrave Square
London SW1X 8PS UK
T(44) 171 235 3505
F(44) 171 235 3565
A network of mostly UK corporate consultants and academics – some activity also in Germany and other European countries. Runs workshops.

www.management.org.uk

Association of Management/International Association of Management

PO Box 64841
Virginia Beach, VA 23469–4841
T(757) 482 2273
F(757) 482 0325
The Association of Management (AoM) and the International Association of Management (IAoM) is a nonprofit professional organization of academicians and practitioners of management founded in 1975. The AoM/IAoM is dedicated to advance the theory and practice of management in the fields of organizational, human resources, information systems and technology, health care and international management, educational administration, leadership and entrepreneurship.

http://www.aom-iaom.com/

Center for Creative Leadership

One Leadership Place
Post Office Box 26300
Greensboro, NC, USA 27438–6300
T(336) 545 2810
F(336) 282 3284
The mission of the Center for Creative Leadership is to advance the understanding, practice, and development of leadership for the benefit of society worldwide.

http://www.ccl.org

Center for Creative Leadership
Avenue Molière 219
1060 Brussels
Belgium
T(32) 2 346 4201
F(32) 2 346 4137
European HQ of its American parent. Runs the well-known Leadership
Development Program.

http://www.ccl.org

Center for Leadership Studies
Vestal Parkway East
PO Box 6015
Binghamton, NY 13902–6015
T(607) 777 3007
The Center for Leadership Studies is a not-for-profit research and educa-
tional institution organized by Binghamton University, State University
of New York, in 1987. Our mission is to contribute to the under-
standing and to identify the importance of a full range of leadership
and its applications.

http://cls.binghamton.edu/

The Centre for Tomorrow's Company
19 Buckingham Street
London
WC2N 6EF
T(44) 020 7930 5150
F(44) 020 7930 5155
We represent a practical vision of sustainable business which makes
sense to shareholders and to society. Our purpose is to explore,
with business, the fundamentals of success and to develop throughout
business better ways of sustaining success.

http://www.tomorrowscompany.com/

The Conference Board Inc.
845 Third Avenue
New York 10022–6679

T(212) 759 0900
F(212) 980 7014

The Conference Board Europe
Chausee de La Hulpe, 130, Box 11
B-1000 Brussels, Belgium
T(32) 2 675 5405
F(32) 2 675 0395
The Conference Board is the world's leading business membership and research organization, connecting senior executives from more than 2900 enterprises in over 60 nations. A not-for-profit, non-advocacy organization.

Provides high-level networking opportunities for more than 13,000 executives through its worldwide conferences, councils, and meetings. It also provides a wide range of reports on best business practices, and economic and public policy issues.

http://www.conference-board.org/index.htm

Cranfield School of Management
Cranfield, Bedfordshire, MK43 0AL
UK
T(44) 1234 751122
F(44) 1234 751806
Postgraduate university. Public and tailored offerings.

www.cranfield.ac.uk

European Association for Personnel Management
T(33-1) 45 63 03 65
F(+33-1) 42 56 41 15
The Association forms an umbrella body of national organizations, which represent personnel professionals. It is purely professional and specialist in nature. It is an experience exchange organization without profit-related objectives.

http://www.eapm.org/

European Foundation of Management Development (EFMD)
Rue Washington 40b
1050 Brussels

T(32) 2 648 0385
F(32) 2 646 0768
Membership based. Runs surveys and benchmarking activities with corporate members.

http://efmd.be

Henley Management College
Greenlands
Henley-on-Thames,
Oxfordshire, RG9 3AU
UK
T(44) 1491 571454
F(44) 1491 571635
Independent management college. Is also in the distance education and development market.

www.henleymc.ac.uk

Hong Kong Management Development Centre
T(852) 2836 1825
F(852) 2572 7130
HKMDC's mission is to develop, promote, and extend managerial effectiveness in Hong Kong through the development of new learning tools, which can be effectively applied to improve personal and organizational competitiveness.

http://www.mdchk.com/mdc.asp

Indian Society for Applied Behavioral Science
1 Magnolias Road
Poona-411 001
India
T(0129) 541 6901 3
ISABS is a value based institution dedicated to the dignity and autonomy of human beings as individuals in groups, organizations and society at large. ISABS is dedicated to understanding, developing, and applying human process competencies through continuous experimentation, research, and learning related to Applied Behavioral Science.

http://isabs.org

INSEAD

Boulevard de Constance
77305 Fontainebleau Cedex, France
T(33) 160 72 40 00
F(33) 1 60 74 55 00
Writers, researchers, consultants on leadership, strategy, and marketing for the executive/senior management development market. Offers courses of 3–4 weeks' duration, tailored offerings and MBAs.
www.insead.fr

Institute of Management

Management House
Cottingham Road, Corby, Northamptonshire NN17 1TT
UK
T(44) 1536 204222
F(44) 1536 201651
Practical general management focus with open and tailored programs. UK market.
www.inst-mgt.org.uk

Institute of Personnel and Development (IPD)

IPD House, Camp Road
London SW19 4UX
T(44) 181 946 9100
F(44) 181 879 7000
Well-recognized professional body and network in the UK. Publishes journals and research reports. Runs courses for HR professionals and general managers.
www.ipd.uk

International Association of Business Communicators

One Hallidie Plaza, Suite 600
San Francisco, CA 94102
T(415) 544 4700.
F(415) 544 4747
IABC is the leading resource for effective communication. They help people and organizations achieve excellence in public relations,

employee communication, marketing communication, public affairs, and other forms of communication.

http://www.iabc.com/about/aboutiab.htm

International Institute for Management Development (IMD)

Ch de Bellerive 23, PO Box 915
CH 1001 Lausanne, Switzerland
T(41) 21 618 0111
F(41) 21 618 0707
Business school. Runs programs in leadership, general management and strategy – offers 3-4 week long public programs and tailored offerings. MBA and EMBA degrees and open enrollment programs are also offered.

http://www.imd.ch

International Leadership Association

James MacGregor Burns Academy of Leadership
University of Maryland
College Park, Maryland, 20742-7715
T(301) 405 5218
F(301) 405 6402
The International Leadership Association with headquarters at the James MacGregor Burns Academy of Leadership at the University of Maryland was established to foster the sharing of ideas, research, and successful practices for leadership practitioners and scholars worldwide.

http://www.academy.umd.edu/ILA

London Business School

Sussex Place
Regent's Park, London NW1 4SA
T(44) 171 262 5050
F(44) 171 724 7875
Postgraduate university. Also provides international short courses in leadership and strategic skills development.

www.lbs.co.uk

Management Centre Europe
rue de l'Aqueduc 118
B-1050 Brussels
Belgium
T(32) 2 543 21 00
F(32) 2 543 24 00
The European arm of the American Management Association, it provides public conferences, seminars and special events in all aspects of business for middle managers.
www.mce.be

NTL/Institute for Applied Behavioral Science
300 North Lee Street, Suite 300
Alexandria, VA 22314–2607
T(703) 548 8840
F(704) 684 1256
National Training Labs was one of the first social science based organizations to further personal and organizational development. Primarily it helps participants learn about themselves and the dynamics of groups through experiential learning techniques.
http://www.ntl.org

Organization Development Network
71 Valley Street
Suite 301
South Orange, NJ 07079–2825
T(973) 763 7337
F(973) 763 7488
The Organization Development Network is a value-based community that supports its members in their work in human organization and systems development, and offers leadership and scholarship to the profession.
http://www.odnet.org/

Singapore Institute of Management
461 Clementi Road
Singapore 599491

T(65) 462 9262
F(65) 462 5751
SIM, an independent, not-for-profit professional organization founded in 1964, is dedicated to enhancing managerial and organizational effectiveness in Singapore.
   http://www2.sim.edu.sg/infgd/simmain.nsf

Society for Human Resource Management

1800 Duke Street
Alexandria, Virginia 22314 USA
T(703) 548 3440
F(703) 535 6490
The Society for Human Resource Management (SHRM), provides continued professional development, promotes national networking, and generally advances the interests of the profession.
   http://www.shrm.org/

BIBLIOGRAPHY

Conger, Jay and Benjamin, Beth (1999) *Building Leaders: How Successful Companies Develop the Next Generation*. Jossey-Bass, San Francisco, CA.

Culbertson, Samuel A. (1996) *Mind-Set Management: The Heart of Leadership*. Oxford University Press, New York.

Elkington, John (1998) *Cannibals With Forks: The Triple Bottom Line of 21st Century Business*. New Society Publishers, Gabriola Island BC, Canada.

Friedman, Thomas L. (1999) *The Lexus and the Olive Tree: Understanding Globalization*. Farrar Straus Giroux, New York.

Goman, Carol (2000) *The Human Side of High Tech: Lessons From the Technology Frontier*. Wiley, New York.

Harris, Philip R. and Moran, Robert T. (2001) *Managing Cultural Differences: Leadership Strategies for a New World of Business*, 5th edn. Butterworth-Heinemann, Woburn, MA.

Hickman, Gill Robinson (ed.) (1998) *Leading Organizations: Perspectives for a New Era*. Sage, Thousand Oaks, CA.

Kets de Vries, Manfred F.R. and Florent-Treacy, Elizabeth (1999) *The New Global Leaders: Richard Branson, Percy Barnevik and David Simon*. Jossey-Bass, San Francisco, CA.

Klein, Naomi (1999) *No Logo: Taking Aim at the Brand Bullies*. Picador, New York.

Korten, David (1995) *When Corporations Rule the World*. Berrett-Koehler, San Francisco, CA.

Matsushita, Konosuke (1984) *Not For Bread Alone: A Business Ethos, A Management Ethic*. PHP Institute, Kyoto, Japan.

McCauley, Cynthia D., Moxley, Russ, S. and Van Velsor, Ellen (eds) (1998) *Handbook of Leadership Development*. Jossey-Bass, San Francisco, CA.

Salmon, Robert (1996) *The Future of Management: All Roads Lead to Man*. Blackwell, Oxford (Translated from *Tous les Chemins Mènent à l'Homme* (1994) Interéditions, Paris).

Schwartz, Peter and Gibb, Blair (1999) *When Good Companies Do Bad Things*. John Wiley, New York.

Senge, Peter (1990) *The Fifth Discipline*. Currency/Doubleday, New York.

Simons, George F., Vasquez, Carmen, and Harris, Philip R. (1993) *Transcultural Leadership: Empowering the Diverse Workforce*, Gulf Publishing, Houston.

Semler, Ricardo (1993) *Maverick: The Success Story Behind the World's Most Unusual Workplace*. Warner Books, New York.

Trompenaars, Alfons and Hampden-Turner, Charles (2001) *21 Leaders for the 21st Century*. McGraw-Hill, New York.

A SAMPLING OF MAGAZINES AND JOURNALS OF SIGNIFICANCE TO GLOBAL LEADERS

» *Business 2.0* – Focuses on how the Internet and e-business are changing and what best practices they create. http://www.business2.com

» *Business Week* – General business weekly. http://www.businessweek.com/

» *The Economist* – UK business news weekly with extensive world coverage. http://www.economist.com/

» *Fast Company* – An up-tempo approach to business success, change, leadership with a focus on personalities, innovation, and creativity. http://www.fastcompany.com

» *Financial Times* (UK) – Business daily with full European business news coverage but focus on UK. One of its unique features is a special section for expats highlighting issues about working and living abroad. http://news.ft.com

» *Forbes* – This business bi-weekly focuses on entrepreneurship among mid-size companies and reports about management issues among larger businesses. http://www.forbes.com/

» *Fortune* – Focuses on big business à la the Fortune 500 with special emphasis on the top 25. http://www.fortune.com/

» *The Futurist* – A beautique journal of the Futurist society, it surveys trends that influence society and has a global perspective. http://www.wfs.org/futurist.htm

» *Harvard Business Review* – Published monthly, this is the primary vehicle for Harvard faculty and graduates (and some non-Harvard related writers) to introduce their latest research in a fashion that is directed to practitioners at the highest corporate levels. http://www.hbsp.harvard.edu/hbr/index.html

» *Journal of Leadership Studies* – A practitioner and teacher oriented quarterly journal of leadership. http://www.baker.edu/departments/leadership/jls-main.htm

» *Leader to Leader* – This quarterly published by the Drucker Center for Non-Profit Management focuses on top management issues of importance to leaders in all organizations. http://www.drucker.org/leaderbooks/121/index.html

» *Management Today* (UK) – Monthly publication focusing on top management in the largest organizations in the UK market. http://www.clickmt.com/index.cfm

» *Management Today* (Singapore) – Published by the Singapore Institute of Management, it is directed at middle managers with a practical how-to approach. Also informs readers about professional events of interest in Singapore and about the Institute's courses. http://www2.sim.edu.sg/infgd/tdmmag.nsf/pages/today's+manager

» *New York Times* – Daily from New York it strives to be the newspaper of record for the US. http://www.nytimes.com/

» *Sloan Management Review* – SMR focuses on corporate strategy, organizational change, and management of technology and innovation, and is published quarterly. http://mitsloan.mit.edu/smr/index.html

» *Wall Street Journal* – Daily from New York. It strives to be the paper of record for business news in the US. http://public.wsj.com/home.html

» *Workforce* – This is directed to HR professionals and covers workforce trends and issues with frequent global supplements. http://www.workforce.com/section/04/

Ten Steps to Making Global Leadership Work

There are three components to becoming an effective global leader. First, preparation; learning about yourself and developing the insights, experiences and skills needed to succeed. Second, execution; being able to influence others to achieve your mutual objectives and realize the organization's vision. Third, evaluation and continuous learning. In all, these components consist of 10 steps toward mastery of the principles of global leadership.

1 Have a clear understanding of what is being done and why, and how it fits in with the vision of the organization.
2 Understand the tactics for achieving and maintaining leadership.
3 Understand that you must adjust your behavior when working with people from different backgrounds, cultures, mindsets.
4 Be clear about the organization's vision, mission, and values.
5 Learn to manage across time and space.
6 Understand the Big Picture and how globalization will impact you.
7 Communicate fully.
8 Develop others.
9 Conduct a personal assessment and accept feedback.
10 Stay fit for the job by practicing continuous learning.

"Sooner or later, if human society is to evolve – indeed, if it is to survive – we must match our lives to our new knowledge."

Marilyn Ferguson

There are three components to becoming an effective global leader. The first is preparation; learning about yourself and developing the insights, experiences, and skills needed to succeed. The second is execution; being able to influence others to achieve your mutual objectives and realize the organization's vision. The third is evaluation and continuous learning. In all these components there are 10 steps toward mastery of the principles of global leadership.

PREPARING FOR GLOBAL LEADERSHIP

Intrapersonal

Step 1: To lead others one must have an understandable purpose related to the tasks at hand, a clear understanding of what is being done and why, and how it fits in with the vision of the organization. And of course this must be communicated clearly.

To accomplish this it is important to understand oneself and how strengths and weaknesses impact interpersonal relationships. It is also important to understand the difference between what's best for the organization and oneself, and one's motivations for influencing others. The inner world of the successful leader is a reflective one with a focus on developing the EI (emotional intelligence) and its five components: self-awareness; self-regulation; motivation; empathy; and social skill.

Becoming one's own best coach requires introspection, the ability for dispassionate observation, a form of detachment from the dynamics of the immediate relationship or other activity, to assess the moment's meaning and what can be learned, reinforced, or extinguished.

Interpersonal

Step 2: Understand the tactics for achieving and maintaining leadership. Remember the following.

» Build solid relationships with targeted followers.
» Be responsive to others in order to build shared social capital.

» Communicate freely to create a reputation of straightforwardness and trustworthiness.
» Develop listening skills that demonstrate others are heard accurately.
» Motivate the group with good cheer.
» Clearly help others create success and build on it.
» Defend and promote the group's interest but not at the expense of the organization.
» Build cohesiveness among team members and colleagues through the practice of positive reinforcement of cooperative efforts.
» Idealize the norms, values, and expectations of the group but be able to learn from experience.
» Have confidence but remain flexible.
» Maintain frequent contact with others as a reminder of your willingness to help them and your concern for their success.
» Identify other informal leaders and build coalitions with them.

Intercultural

Step 3: Understand that you must adjust your behavior when working with people from different backgrounds, cultures, mindsets. This becomes most obvious when you are physically in another culture but this is increasingly a fact of life wherever you are.

Reflect on the results of the GLOBE study

For top managers, characteristics such as being innovative, visionary, persuasive, long-term oriented, diplomatic, and courageous are considered more important than for lower level managers. Attributes of effective lower level managers are higher on characteristics such as attention to subordinates, team building, and being participative. Also, such social and participative characteristics are deemed more important to be an effective lower level manager than to be an effective top manager.

Being trustworthy, communicative, and calm are considered equally important for both types of managers. Being inspirational, rational, and a confidence builder are also found to be effective.

Being communicative, inspirational, and a confidence builder were endorsed almost equally for both top and lower level leadership. Although the universally endorsed characteristics such as being a visionary and diplomatic were endorsed for both types of leadership the importance of these attributes is seen as higher for top managers. Finally, team building was seen as more important at lower levels.

The combined results of the major GLOBE study and the follow-up study demonstrate that several attributes reflecting charismatic/transformational leadership are universally endorsed as contributing to outstanding leadership. These include motive arouser, foresight, encouraging, communicative, trustworthy, dynamic, positive, confidence builder, and motivational.

These findings are part of an ongoing research effort in over 60 countries to understand the similarities and differences in leadership effectiveness among them.[1]

Of course the best way to prepare for any overseas assignment, whether for one day or for an indefinite period of time, is to become open and accepting of differences, to know the distinction between one's personal preferences and functional requirements of the moment. A helpful tool to discover how to behave in a different environment and to think through appropriate behavioral changes that might be required is the culture management matrix discussed in Chapter 7. It helps you focus your attention on how aspects of a culture impact your functioning in a leadership role.

EXECUTION: THE PRACTICE OF GLOBAL LEADERSHIP

Step 4: Be clear about the organization's vision, mission, and values. It is important to establish an appropriate vision and mission with a supportive set of values that work worldwide. Whether it is the Nokia Way, the H-P Way, the Fujitsu Way or the Bata Way, an organization leverages its resources through focusing on a single vision of what its purpose is and a set of values understood by each employee. This enables people to make decisions and to deduce how they can contribute to the organization's objectives. This is not just a good idea. It is essential to create psychological and decision making efficiencies. It's simple. When everyone knows their purpose and how they fit into achieving the organization's purpose, there is little need for oversight and bureaucracy. In a world that requires speedy innovation and decisions to be made at the point of customer contact, a clear vision, mission, and set of values serve as guidance to each person on how best to serve the organization.

Step 5: Manage time and space. The greatest challenge to a global leader is influencing others through time and space. Not being face-to-face is one limitation, team members having asynchronous work schedules and being in distant locations are additional limitations – both of which are compounded by cross-cultural issues. Having a clear sense of purpose, an understanding of the mission and vision and values, and communicating these ideas frequently reinforces the team's goals, honors successes, and encourages learning. This is vital. Connecting your network through an in-house intranet or other form of groupware to manage data, conversations, and schedules would be a necessary task for a global leader.

Step 6: Understand the big picture. Consider how an audit of the triple bottom line will impact your organization and the leadership role. Recall that the triple bottom line is attention to profit, bottom line one: attention to any environmental impact due to your business presence, bottom line two; and your relationships with all other constituencies especially in regard to social issues such as human rights, workers' rights, and relations with the community, bottom line three.

As a manager-leader in your organization determining an appropriate societal role in overseas locations and developing a mindfulness about the triple bottom line – basically understanding the big picture surrounding your organization's presence – is essential to succeed cross-culturally and also to avoid getting trapped in the anti-globalization backlash.

Step 7: Communicate fully. If it is accepted that distance compounds the difficulties in relationship building and requires more attention, and that cross-cultural relationship building increases the hazards and complexities in those relationships, there are really only two things you can do about it – increase your understanding of others and communicate fully with those in your network. Keep the contact alive, inform everyone of what is happening, why, what is expected of them, how it fits into the team effort and especially how their contributions are appreciated. If you can, arrange face-to-face meetings as frequently as possible though meeting on the web is an obvious necessity for most of the work of your global team.

Try also to maintain a team journal – a record of the processes used by the team and their impact on both individuals and the team's accomplishments. This could be an assigned role for one of the members of the team who, by keeping the journal, also serves as the historian for the team helping it keep track of the collective conversation and progress.

Step 8: Develop others. Use an in-house leadership development process that keeps the leadership pipeline open and available throughout the organization. Peer to peer coaching, mentoring by top executives of the high potential middle managers, skills development opportunities for everyone who works with others and action learning projects that focus on personal leadership behavior are a few of the components of a program to insure a steady supply of talent when and where the organization needs it.

Evaluation: knowing you are succeeding

Step 9: Personal assessment and feedback. The purpose of 360-degree evaluation is to use the input from subordinates, colleagues, customers, and bosses to create an overall picture of your performance. It is used for training and development purposes as well as for personal feedback. It should not be used for promotional or pay determinations.

The spirit of 360-degree feedback – getting a perspective on one's performance from all who interact with the individual – is extremely valuable for self and team development. It provides the individual with the data regarding how his or her behavior impacts others and what's working well and what's not. This is one of the most powerful development tools, especially when combined with focused feedback from a peer coach.

Step 10: Continuous learning: staying fit for the job. Keeping up, checking in, seeking new opportunities to understand different perspectives from around the globe are important. Take advantage of new challenges and responsibilities to work with people from varied backgrounds whether at home or abroad, know what impact you and your organization have in another country and among people of diverse backgrounds. This knowledge is crucial for the improvement of organizational and personal performance. Change is forcing us to learn more, faster. And keeping up is a requirement to maintain one's personal employability as well as effectiveness on the job now.

Developing the skills to work with people anywhere on the planet, to see the earth as a single home market and to understand the forces that are at work when operating globally is an exciting and challenging aspect of working in an organization today.

NOTE

1 House, Robert J. "A Brief History of GLOBE," see http://www.mgm-t3.ucalgary.ca/eb/globe.nsf/index

Frequently Asked Questions (FAQs)

Q1: How does a global organization differ from a multinational organization?

A: See Chapter 1: Introduction to Global Leaders.

Q2: What is the difference between global leadership and leadership?

A: See Chapter 2: Definition of Terms.

Q3: How can one prepare for global leadership?

A: See Chapter 3: The Evolution of Global Leadership, particularly Global Leadership and Organizational Effectiveness. Also see Chapter 7: Global Leadership in Practice, especially Preparing Global Leaders.

Q4: How does one lead a team whose members and resources are located around the world?

A: See Chapter 4: The E-Dimension, especially the Box: Making Virtual Teams Work.

Q5: How can I deal with the backlash to globalization?

A: See Chapter 5: The Global Dimension.

Q6: What issues will emerge to confront the global leader?

A: See Chapter 6: The State of the Art of Global Leadership, especially The Four Challenges Faced by Organizations in Preparing Global Leaders

Q7: What companies exemplify best practice in global leadership?

A: See Chapter 7: Global Leadership in Practice.

Q8: Who are the leading experts on leadership?

A: See Chapter 8: Key Concepts and Thinkers in Global Leadership.

Q9: What resources are available to learn more about global leadership?

A: See Chapter 9: Resources, which includes a selected bibliography, selected professional organizations, and publications of relevance to global leaders.

Q10: What is the impact of the Internet on global leadership?

A: See Chapter 4: The E-Dimension of Global Leadership.

Acknowledgments

Thanks to Tom Brown, John Willig, Stuart Crainer, and Allyson Villars for their support and encouragement, and to the many researchers and practitioners working in the field of global leadership who have made this volume possible.

Index